MEGABITES
GLADIATORS
RIVETING READS FOR CURIOUS KIDS

M E G A B I T E S
GLADIATORS
RIVETING READS FOR CURIOUS KIDS

By
John Malam

Consultants
Guy de la Bédoyère, Peter Chrisp

Penguin Random House

Second Edition

DK London

Senior Editor Sam Atkinson
Managing Editor Lisa Gillespie
Managing Art Editor Owen Peyton Jones
Production Editor Gillian Reid
Senior Production Controller
Meskerem Berhane
Jacket Design Development Manager
Sophia MTT
Publisher Andrew Macintyre
Associate Publishing Director Liz Wheeler
Art Director Karen Self
Publishing Director Jonathan Metcalf

DK Delhi

Senior Editor Sreshtha Bhattacharya
Senior Art Editor Vikas Chauhan
Editor Upamanyu Das
Art Editor Sanya Jain
Managing Editor Kingshuk Ghoshal
Managing Art Editor Govind Mittal
Senior DTP Designers Neeraj Bhatia,
Shanker Prasad
DTP Designer Jaypal Chauhan
Pre-Production Manager Balwant Singh
Production Manager Pankaj Sharma
Jacket Designers Suhita Dharamjit,
Pooja Pipil

First Edition

Project Editor Steve Setford
Project Art Editor Peter Radcliffe
Senior Editor Fran Jones
Senior Art Editor Stefan Podhorodecki
Category Publisher Jayne Parsons
Managing Art Editor Jacquie Gulliver
Picture Researcher Sarah Pownall
DK Picture Library Sally Hamilton, Sarah Mills, Rose Horridge
Production Erica Rosen
DTP Designer Siu Yin Ho

This edition published in 2020
First published as *Gladiator* in Great Britain in 2002 by
Dorling Kindersley Limited
DK, One Embassy Gardens, 8 Viaduct Gardens, London, SW11 7BW

Copyright © 2002, 2020 Dorling Kindersley Limited
A Penguin Random House Company
10 9 8 7 6 5 4 3 2
003-318467-Nov/2020

All rights reserved.
No part of this publication may be reproduced, stored in or introduced into
a retrieval system, or transmitted, in any form, or by any means (electronic,
mechanical, photocopying, recording, or otherwise), without the prior
written permission of the copyright owner.

A CIP catalogue record for this book is available from the British Library.
ISBN: 978-0-2414-3754-4

Printed and bound in the UK

For the curious
www.dk.com

This book was made with Forest Stewardship
Council ™ certified paper – one small step in
DK's commitment to a sustainable future.
For more information go to
www.dk.com/our-green-pledge

CONTENTS

INTRODUCTION

Picture the scene: a huge stadium in ancient Rome is packed with a noisy, excited crowd. They are here to watch gladiators fight to the death. Suddenly, the spectators fall silent as a fighter falls to the ground wounded. Then they start to shout in Latin *"Iugula!"* It means "Kill him!"

It's hard to imagine that anything so horrible, so bloodthirsty, could ever have happened. But to the Romans, the spectacle of highly trained fighters attacking each other with swords, daggers, lances, tridents, and nets was simply great entertainment!

Although gladiators are long gone, the fascination with these Roman fighters is as strong as ever. Today, crowds still like to watch them perform – not in blood-soaked stadiums but in plush cinemas, where actors play the part of Roman fighters. As we watch the latest blockbuster film, packed with

THIS CARVING OF TWO WOMEN FIGHTING SHOWS THAT WOMEN, AS WELL AS MEN, FOUGHT AS GLADIATORS.

special effects,
or play the latest
computer game,
we can imagine
that we've travelled
back in time to the
world the Romans knew.

But what was that
world really like? That's
where you'll find this book
helpful. You'll travel through
the magnificent city that was
ancient Rome, in Italy. You'll find
out about the Romans' everyday
lives, their emperors and gods,
and their soldiers and empire. But
most of all, you'll get to know the
gladiators whose blood was spilled
in the Colosseum, Rome's most
awe-inspiring stadium. It could
seat 50,000 spectators, and might
even be flooded for mock sea battles. Yet it was just
one of more than 230 great amphitheatres, which the
Romans built across their empire from North Africa to
the eastern Mediterranean.

But enough introduction. As the Romans would have
said "Mox nox in rem!" – "Let's get this show on the road!"

John Malam

DEADLY HEROES

Gladiators were the superstars of their time. They were adored by their fans and rewarded with large sums of money – just like today's stars of music, sport, and film. But there was one crucial difference between gladiators and modern crowd-pleasers – these Roman entertainers killed one another. Cold-blooded killing was their job.

A taste for violence

Gladiators were a Roman fashion – the world has seen nothing like them before or since. In towns and cities throughout the Roman Empire, arenas of all sizes were built to stage shows for the public – especially gladiatorial games. These violent, bloody contests were usually the most popular event in a town's social calendar, a chance for people to see their heroes in action. Roman audiences were as happy to watch gladiators spilling each other's blood as they were to watch actors perform a comedy play at the theatre. The Romans thought that gladiator fights were a perfectly acceptable form of entertainment. It was gory but glamorous, and they loved it. It's only later generations – and that includes us – who think of them as horrible acts of violence, the nastiest, cruelest blood-sport ever invented.

Bringers of good luck

The Roman liking for watching fighting and killing in public lasted for some 500 years. It's not surprising, then, that gladiators played such a big part in Roman society. All manner of superstitions and beliefs grew up around them. For example, during a marriage ceremony it was the custom on the wedding day for the bride to part her hair with the tip of a spear – and if it had belonged to a gladiator killed in the arena, she would be blessed

THIS PICTURE CAPTURES THE DRAMA OF THE ARENA. A FALLEN GLADIATOR LOOKS TO THE CROWD TO SEE IF THEY WILL SPARE HIS LIFE. THEIR "THUMBS DOWN" RESPONSE SIGNALS THAT THE LOSER SHOULD DIE.

with good luck. Perhaps the meaning of this strange act was to drive out harmful spirits believed to be tangled in the bride's hair. Customs such as this show how fascinating gladiators were to ordinary Roman people.

Feared fighters

The truth is, underneath this fascination with gladiators lay a tremendous fear of them.

It was because gladiators were professional fighters, trained in the brutal art of committing public executions, that they scared most Romans.

Despite this, the Romans loved watching these powerful fighters battle it out in the arena from the safety of their ringside seats. Children played with pottery gladiator dolls, and people had pictures of them in their homes – on

THE LAST GLADIATOR CONTESTS TOOK PLACE MORE THAN 1,600 YEARS AGO.

lamps, tableware, and mosaics. These often showed real fights, with the names of the gladiators written beside them. We know from the writings of Pliny the Elder that gladiators were a popular subject in Roman art for many generations.

THIS IS A TOMBSTONE OF A RETIARIUS – A GLADIATOR WHO FOUGHT WITH A NET AND A THREE-PRONGED SPEAR CALLED A TRIDENT.

Position in society

Gladiators generally held a low position in Roman society. Many were prisoners captured in war, or criminals condemned to fight. But there were also those who willingly became gladiators. Some were desperate or in debt, knowing that they would be taken care of. Others loved to fight, and hoped to win the cheers of the crowd. When a free person became a gladiator, they gave up their legal rights.

Despite their low position in society, gladiators were not short of admirers. Those who fought well and lived to see another day attracted fans, many of whom were women. We know this from the

IN THIS SCENE FROM A MOSAIC MADE IN THE 4TH CENTURY CE, A VICTORIOUS GLADIATOR STANDS OVER THE BODY OF HIS VICTIM.

WEIRD WORLD

IF A ROMAN MAN HAD A DREAM INVOLVING A TYPE OF GLADIATOR KNOWN AS A *THRAEX*, IT WAS TAKEN AS A SIGN THAT HE WAS GOING TO MARRY A RICH WOMAN!

graffiti people left on the walls of arenas in which their heroes fought.

At the arena in Pompeii, a small Roman town in southern Italy, a gladiator named Celadus was described as a "girls' hero" and a "heart-throb", while another, called Crescens, was hailed as "the boss".

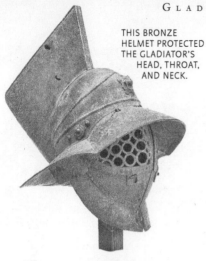

THIS BRONZE HELMET PROTECTED THE GLADIATOR'S HEAD, THROAT, AND NECK.

The emperor-gladiator

You'd be shocked if you saw your country's leader fighting in public – unless, that is, you were at a gladiatorial contest in Rome in the late 2nd century CE. If you'd gone to the Colosseum, which was the place to see the heroes of the arena, you might have seen the Emperor Commodus fighting as a gladiator. Think about it – the leader of Rome fighting for his life! Gladiators were admired for their bravery. Their daring deeds gripped the public's imagination, and Commodus wanted to be admired in the same way. Although he wanted to fight like a gladiator, he didn't want to die like one. He boasted that he had beaten 12,000 opponents, fighting some 735 times without getting hurt.

GLADIATORS FOUGHT ONE-TO-ONE, AS SHOWN IN THIS MODERN RE-ENACTMENT.

had in Roman society – all the way to the top. But how did Rome's terrifying terminators come about? Well, the story of gladiators goes hand in hand with Rome's development from a cluster of tiny villages into the greatest power of the ancient world.

Ordinary gladiators were lucky if they made it into double figures before biting the dust.

Unfair fights

The secret of Commodus's success was the fact that he was the Emperor. His opponents knew that humiliating him in public would result in their certain death. Commodus also re-enacted popular myths such as the story of Hercules's battle with snake-legged giants. He made some men who had lost their feet play the giants. They had only sponges to throw instead of rocks, and he killed them with a club. He also executed wild animals. During one 14-day bloodbath, he slaughtered 100 bears from the safety of the arena.

Commodus, the emperor-gladiator, is just one example of how much influence gladiators

COMMODUS MODELLED HIMSELF ON HERCULES – THE LEGENDARY STRONGMAN AND SLAYER OF MONSTERS – BY WEARING A LION-SKIN CLOAK AND CARRYING A CLUB.

THE RISE OF ROME

By 100 CE, Rome was the grandest city on Earth and the centre of a massive empire. Home to about 1 million people, it was a fabulous place, with sumptuous palaces, grand statues, magnificent triumphal arches celebrating Rome's victories, and, of course, the Colosseum – the finest gladiator stadium in the Roman Empire. Often, the Roman people wondered how and when it had all begun.

The wolf and the twins
Like many peoples of the ancient world, the Romans made up stories to explain things about themselves and their world. In time, these stories, or myths, became accepted as true facts rather than invented tales.

To explain the origins of their city, the Romans told one of the best-known myths of all time – the story of the twin boys Romulus and Remus.
In the

story, the two boys were thrown into the River Tiber on the instructions of their great-uncle, King Amulius. The king wanted them to die so they would never find out about the cruel things he had done to their family. Amulius was afraid that if they lived they would take revenge on him.

But Romulus and Remus did not die. They were discovered by a she-wolf who fed them with her own milk until a shepherd took them home and brought them up as his own sons. They grew into strong young men, and when they learned about Amulius

WEIRD WORLD
MARCUS AGRIPPA (63–12 BCE) IMPROVED ROME'S WATERWORKS. IN 33 BCE, THE CITY'S GREATEST SEWER WAS CLEANED. AGRIPPA SAILED THROUGH IT IN A BOAT TO INSPECT THE WORK!

they went to his city and killed him – just as he had feared.

Having avenged their family, the brothers decided to build a city of their own, on the banks of the River Tiber. But, like

ROME WAS AT ITS FINEST BETWEEN 100 CE AND 300 CE. AT THE CITY'S HEART WAS THE COLOSSEUM, THE OVAL BUILDING SHOWN IN THIS MODEL.

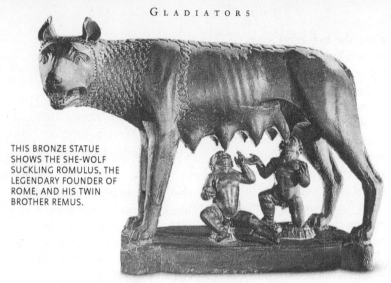

THIS BRONZE STATUE SHOWS THE SHE-WOLF SUCKLING ROMULUS, THE LEGENDARY FOUNDER OF ROME, AND HIS TWIN BROTHER REMUS.

all brothers, they argued – they couldn't decide which of them should be the king or what the city should be called. They fought, and in the struggle Romulus killed Remus. It was left to Romulus to build the city alone, which he named Rome, after himself.

Ancient Romans believed that their city had been founded in 753 BCE, and used this year as the first date in the Roman calendar. In fact, archaeologists have shown that Rome is much older than the Romans believed.

The truth about Rome

The real story of Rome begins 3,000 years ago, some time around 1000 BCE. This was when settlers arrived in a region that ran along the west coast of central Italy. The settlers were farmers, and they recognized that the region's fertile soil would be good for growing their crops and for raising farm animals. They built their villages on the summits of a group of seven low-lying hills, near a

THIS COIN DEPICTS ROMA, THE PATRON GODDESS OF ROME. CITIZENS OF ROME WORSHIPPED HER AND ASKED HER TO PROTECT THEIR CITY.

crossing over the River Tiber, the region's largest river. The villages prospered and grew in size. Within less than 300 years they had spread out across the hilltops, and by about 750 BCE they had joined together to form a town. It was this early town that marked the birth of the city that would later become known as Rome.

The hated kings of Rome

Rome lay in a region of Italy called Latium, which was divided into different city-states (you can think of them as "tribal areas"). The inhabitants of Latium were known as Latins. Immediately to their north was the region of Etruria, the home of a cultured people called the Etruscans. For a time, the Etruscans were the most powerful people in northern Italy. In the 7th century BCE, the Etruscans gained control of Rome, and for about 100 years, the city was ruled by Etruscan kings.

By 509 BCE, the Roman people had had enough of Etruscan rule. They rebelled and threw Tarquin the Proud, the last of the hated Etruscan kings, out of Rome. From then on, Rome was ruled by a group of its leading citizens. It had become a republic – a state

---

A FARMER FROM ROMAN TIMES WOULD STILL RECOGNIZE TODAY'S COUNTRYSIDE NEAR ROME, WITH ITS OLIVE AND CYPRESS TREES, VINEYARDS, AND SMALL FIELDS.

or country governed
by politicians elected by
the people.

From republic to empire

The Roman Republic lasted
for almost 500 years, from
509 BCE to 27 BCE. During this
long time, Rome was ruled
by the Senate – a group of
men who came from leading
Roman families. The senators,
as they were known, pledged
that Rome would never again
be in the hands of just one
powerful person, such as
a king.

Day-to-day decision-
making was left in the
hands of officials known
as magistrates, who were
elected for one year at a
time. The two most important
magistrates were the consuls.
These men had the power to
pass laws and declare war

THE SHADED AREAS ON THIS MAP SHOW
THE GROWTH OF ROMAN TERRITORY.

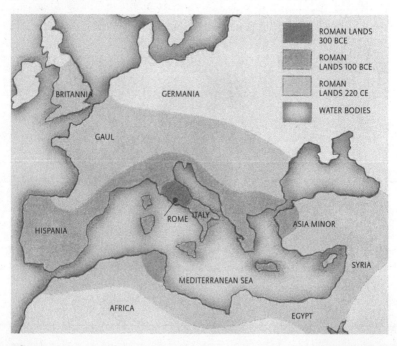

	ROMAN LANDS 300 BCE
	ROMAN LANDS 100 BCE
	ROMAN LANDS 220 CE
	WATER BODIES

BRITANNIA

GERMANIA

GAUL

HISPANIA

ROME ITALY

ASIA MINOR

SYRIA

MEDITERRANEAN SEA

AFRICA

EGYPT

on Rome's enemies. Each consul checked the work of the other, to make sure that neither became too powerful. strong armies led by powerful generals. During the closing years of the Roman Republic,. a civil war broke out between

BY 120 CE, AS MANY AS 50 MILLION PEOPLE LIVED UNDER ROMAN RULE.

The rise of Rome

It was during the years of the Roman Republic that Rome developed into the strongest force in Italy. Rome gradually overpowered Italy's other city-states and brought them under its control. A long series of wars fought against Carthage, a major power based in North Africa, ended in victory for Rome in 146 BCE. This triumph left Rome as the greatest power in the Mediterranean. Over the following 100 years Rome – backed by the might of its army – took control of vast tracts of land, from Spain and Gaul (France) in the west to Greece and Syria in the east.

Civil war!

Rome's rise to power would not have been possible without

DURING THE ROMAN REPUBLIC, POWER LAY IN THE HANDS OF THE SENATORS. EVERY YEAR, THE PEOPLE VOTED TO ELECT CERTAIN SENATORS TO BE GOVERNMENT OFFICIALS.

19

Rome's two most brilliant generals, Pompey the Great (106–48 BCE) and Julius Caesar (100–44 BCE). Caesar defeated have again. A plot was hatched, and Caesar was stabbed to death at a Senate meeting in 44 BCE.

CAESAR WORE A CROWN OF LAUREL LEAVES TO HIDE HIS BALD PATCH!

Pompey, and made himself the dictator of Rome – a single ruler with more power than the magistrates. To the proud Romans, Caesar had become too much like a king – the type of leader they never wanted to

The first emperor

Caesar's death solved nothing. Civil war flared up again as other generals fought to take control. Among them was Octavian (63 BCE–14 CE), the great-nephew of Julius Caesar.

In 31 BCE, Octavian defeated his enemies. He was now the sole ruler of Rome. But Octavian knew that the Senate and the Roman people would never accept this. So, in 27 BCE, he offered to hand his powers back to the Senate, saying it was his way of bringing peace to the Roman world.

It was a clever move and the turning point in Rome's history. The Senate accepted Octavian's offer, but still left him with immense power. He was given a new name, Augustus, which meant the "revered one". He had become the first emperor.

AFTER DEFEATING POMPEY, JULIUS CAESAR (LEFT) MADE HIMSELF THE SOLE RULER OF ROME, BUT MADE MANY ENEMIES BY ACTING LIKE A KING.

CAESAR, STABBED TO DEATH BY 60
SENATORS, FELL AT THE FOOT OF THE
STATUE OF POMPEY, HIS FORMER ENEMY.

The Roman Empire had begun!
For the next 500 years, Rome
was ruled by emperors.

Rome, city of marble
Augustus once said of Rome,
"I inherited it brick and left
it marble". He meant that he
had rebuilt many of the public
buildings, facing them with
marble, as well as paving public
squares with marble. He wasn't
alone. Many of the emperors
who came after him stamped
their own identities on the city,
erecting ever grander buildings
and monuments.

At the heart of Rome was the
Forum – a rectangular space that
became the political, commercial,
religious, and social centre of the
entire Roman world. The Forum
was surrounded by government
buildings, law courts, and temples.
Politicians gave speeches from
platforms in the Forum, listened
to by crowds of
Roman citizens.

To the west
of the Forum
lay the Campus
Martius (Field
of Mars) where
the earliest
gladiator fights
were staged.

UNDER THE NEW
NAME AUGUSTUS,
OCTAVIAN BECAME THE
FIRST ROMAN EMPEROR.
HIS RULE BROUGHT PEACE
TO THE ROMAN WORLD.

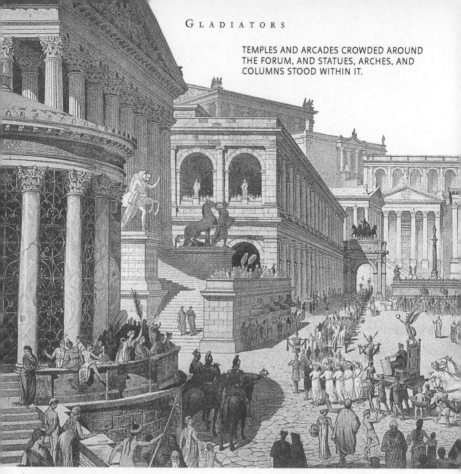

TEMPLES AND ARCADES CROWDED AROUND THE FORUM, AND STATUES, ARCHES, AND COLUMNS STOOD WITHIN IT.

Following a great fire in Rome, which destroyed the amphitheatre in the Campus Martius, Emperor Vespasian built a vast new showground on the east side of the Forum. It was called the Flavian Amphitheatre, and later acquired a new name… the Colosseum.

Bigger and better

Rome continued to grow, and a list of all its buildings was made between 300 CE and 400 CE.

Here's part of what the surveyors recorded. There were 28 libraries, 8 bridges, 11 town squares (fora), 10 basilicas, 19 aqueducts delivering 760 million litres (167 million gallons) of water a day, 1,352 drinking fountains, 11 big bath-houses and 856 small ones, 3 theatres, 29 main roads, 2 race-tracks (circuses), 2 amphitheatres, 36 triumphal arches, 37 gates in the city wall (which was 50 km [31 miles] all round),

by what they saw. To guide them, a "street map", known as the *Forma Urbis*, was put up in a prominent place. Measuring an enormous 18 by 14 m (60 by 45 ft), it was carved onto rectangular marble slabs between 203 CE and 211 CE. Every street, building, room, and staircase in Rome was shown on it.

Unfortunately for us, this unique map got smashed to pieces long ago. Archaeologists have so far found 1,163 pieces of it. But this amounts to a mere 15 per cent of the total, so 85 per cent of the map is still missing. The hunt is on to find the rest of this giant jigsaw!

290 warehouses, 254 cornmills, 1,797 houses owned by wealthy citizens, 46,602 apartments and small houses, and, bottom of the list, 144 public lavatories!

Map of stone
Just like day's great cities, tourists visited Rome and were amazed

EACH YEAR, SEVEN MILLION TOURISTS VISIT THE COLOSSEUM, WHICH STILL TOWERS OVER THE CENTRE OF ROME.

LEGIONARIES AND LEADERS

R ome was one of the world's first superpowers, led by skillful politicians, generals, and emperors. These ambitious leaders were determined to make Rome, and themselves, great. Some succeeded, but others were tyrants who fell out of favour with the people, and with Rome's greatest asset – the army.

Rome's all-conquering army

The Roman army was a truly formidable fighting machine, and its generals were skilled in the crafts of warfare – from hand-to-hand combat to long sieges. They were determined to win at any cost. After one of Julius Caesar's famous battles, he sent a letter to the Senate with the phrase, *"Veni, vidi, vici,"* ("I came, I saw, I conquered"). Led by Caesar

THE TACTICS AND EQUIPMENT OF IMPERIAL ROMAN SOLDIERS ARE RECREATED HERE BY DEDICATED MODERN ENTHUSIASTS.

THIS IS A REPLICA OF A GIANT CATAPULT CALLED AN ONAGER. IT THREW HEAVY ROCKS OVER LONG DISTANCES, AND WAS USED BY THE ROMAN ARMY TO BATTER DOWN AN ENEMY'S DEFENCES.

and other generals, Rome's brave soldiers won victory after victory, defeating enemies and conquering foreign lands.

Roman soldiers were all men and were highly trained and well-equipped. Those who had the misfortune to face them in battle were lucky if they survived

Organizing the army

Good organization was the key to the army's success. At first, the whole of the Roman army was known as the *legio* (legion), a Latin word for levy, meaning "to raise an army". Later, during the 5th century BCE, the army was split into divisions, also

THE LARGEST CATAPULTS COULD HURL ROCKS 500 M (1,600 FT).

to fight another day – unless, that is, they were taken prisoner. If this happened, they were likely to end up as one of the next generation of gladiators, many of whom were prisoners-of-war.

called legions, each containing a large number of legionaries (foot soldiers). There was also a small cavalry force, but it was never as important as the infantry.

25

ROMAN ARMOUR CHANGED OVER THE CENTURIES. THIS IS A REPLICA OF ARMOUR WORN IN THE LATE 1ST CENTURY CE.

Reforming general

In the 1st century BCE, Gaius Marius (157–86 BCE), a leading politician and general, introduced some major reforms to the military. One was to make the troops full-time soldiers, rather than part-timers. Another was to let poor men join the army. Also, soldiers were to be paid and equipped by the state for the first time. The changes brought about by Marius helped the Roman army become the supreme fighting force of its time.

Anatomy of a legion

From the 1st century CE, a legion consisted of 5,500 men. It was divided into 10 cohorts, plus cavalry and officers. The first cohort contained the legion's 800 finest soldiers – its crack troops. The other nine cohorts each had 480 men. Within the cohorts, soldiers were split into groups called centuries, each of which had 80 men (at one time it was 100 men).

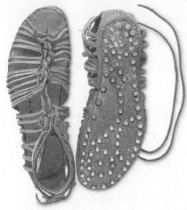

SOLDIERS MARCHED 30 KM (20 MILES) A DAY. BOOTS WITH HARD-WEARING IRON STUDS ON THE SOLES WERE ESSENTIAL.

Weapons and armour

During the 2nd century CE, when the army reached its greatest size with some 380,000 men, legionaries were issued with a fairly standard kit. Weapons included a dagger (*pugio*), a short sword (*gladius*), and a heavy javelin (*pilum*), the tip of which would bend on impact, making it impossible to be thrown back by the enemy.

Legionaries wore strips of flexible metal and

Centuries were themselves broken down into the smallest units of all – squads of eight soldiers who would share a tent together while they were on campaign. Each century was led by a centurion. Above him were six officers, called tribunes, who advised the legion's commanding officer, the legate.

THE SHORT SWORD WAS THE LEGIONARY'S MAIN WEAPON FOR CLOSE-RANGE FIGHTING. THIS ONE IS IN ITS SCABBARD. THE JAVELIN WAS THROWN FROM A DISTANCE.

leather armour on their bodies. Metal helmets protected the soldiers' heads, cheeks, and necks. Large rectangular shields deflected enemy missiles, and they could also be overlapped to form all-round protection for a group of men. On the march, the legionary carried not

WEIRD WORLD

ON THE MARCH, LEGIONARIES CARRIED EQUIPMENT – WEIGHING BETWEEN 27 AND 40 KG (60 AND 90 LB) – ON THEIR SHOULDERS. THEY WERE NICKNAMED "MARIUS'S MULES", AFTER THE GENERAL WHO HAD IMPROVED THE ROMAN ARMY.

only his weapons and armour, but also a weighty set of digging tools, which he needed when the legion stopped to make camp.

Conditions of service

Life was tough for a legionary. Some complained of harsh treatment. For those sent to the farthest outposts of the Roman Empire, the weather was an added problem. For

HADRIAN'S WALL IN NORTHERN BRITAIN WAS A FRONTIER OF THE ROMAN EMPIRE. BEYOND IT LIVED NON-ROMAN PEOPLE. THE ROMANS CALLED THEM BARBARIANS.

example, one soldier stationed in northern Britain asked for woollen socks, underpants, and sandals – presumably he found the cool, wet climate very different from the one in his homeland, wherever that was.

Legionaries joined the army for between 20 and 25 years. They were not officially allowed to marry, but many did. They learned new skills and usually received regular pay, as well as good medical treatment. On leaving the army they were given land, although this was eventually changed to a gift of

WEIRD WORLD
THE WORST PUNISHMENT FACED BY A COHORT WAS THE PRACTICE OF DECIMATION, WHEN THE SOLDIERS LINED UP AND EVERY TENTH MAN WAS CLUBBED OR STONED TO DEATH. ("DECI" MEANS TEN, AS IN THE WORD DECIMAL.)

money equal to 12 years' pay. After completing their military service, men were free to return to their homes, but many chose to stay in the countries where they had been posted.

Citizens and non-citizens
All legionaries were Roman citizens – men who had rights that others did not (such as being able to vote in elections). However, not all soldiers were legionaries. Many were non-citizens who came from the 40 or so provinces (territories) of the Roman Empire. Known as auxiliaries, these provincial troops were specialist fighters who served as archers, slingers, and cavalry. These soldiers played a vital role in defending the borders of the empire and the millions of people who lived within it. At the end of his service, an auxiliary soldier was granted Roman citizenship, which improved his status in society.

The emperor's bodyguards
Augustus, the first Roman emperor, created a special group of soldiers known as

ON PARADE, THE PRAETORIAN GUARD WORE DECORATED ARMOUR. AT OTHER TIMES THEY WORE PLAIN ARMOUR.

the Praetorian Guard. It was a force of up to 10,000 carefully chosen men, whose duty was to protect the emperor from injury and rebellions. The Praetorians lived in their own barracks on the outskirts of Rome. Emperors after Augustus continued to use the Praetorians as their personal bodyguards, but as time passed the political power of these elite soldiers grew. If they disliked an emperor, they might murder him and replace him with a leader they preferred.

A risky job

It was the custom for Roman soldiers to cheer a victorious general, calling out *"Imperator!"*, meaning "our commander" or "our emperor". An ambitious general might take this as a sign that the army wanted

him to be emperor. If he felt he had enough support, both from the troops and from the Senate, he could make a bid to replace an unpopular emperor. For this reason, an emperor

buy meat from the market! However, a handful of emperors, including Trajan, were great leaders, loved by their people and dreaded by their enemies. It was during

THE PRAETORIANS MURDERED AT LEAST 15 ROMAN EMPERORS.

could never afford to fall out with the army, and there was always a chance that one of the generals was plotting to overthrow him.

Emperors good and bad
About 175 men claimed the title of emperor during the 500 years of the Roman Empire. Between 235 and 284 CE, there were 21 official emperors, and many more who tried to seize power, but failed. Almost all died violent deaths, usually at the hands of their own soldiers.

Some emperors were tyrants, feared for their cruelty. Caligula, for example, had prisoners killed, and then fed them to the wild beasts kept at the arena, because it was cheaper to do this than to

Trajan's reign that the Roman Empire reached its greatest extent, and many new buildings were put up in Rome.

ON TRAJAN'S COLUMN IN ROME THERE IS A RELIEF CARVING THAT SHOWS SCENES FROM THE EMPEROR'S BATTLE VICTORIES.

CRUEL COLOSSEUM

Rome's mighty Colosseum opened to the public in the year 80 CE. To celebrate the event, 100 days of gory games were held there. Scores of gladiators were killed and up to 5,000 animals a day were butchered. This was only the start. For the next 400 blood-stained years, the Colosseum was to be the Roman world's premier killing-ground.

CORRIDOR

SEATING

An awe-inspiring arena
No one knows who designed the Colosseum, but one thing's certain – it was built to last. It took about 10 years to put up the massive oval-shaped arena, which was fast work in those days. The finished building stood some 50 m (164 ft) high and measured 188 by 156 m (616 by 512 ft). Hard-wearing materials were used. The foundations and upper levels were formed from concrete, the outer wall used travertine (a whitish limestone),

and the tiers of seating were made from white marble, which was transported by ship along the River Tiber. Blocks of stone were moved by treadmill cranes. These were operated by workers who walked, like hamsters, inside huge wheels. As the wheels turned they pulled on ropes that raised and lowered the building stones into place.

Seats, safety, and sun

The Colosseum could seat about 45,000 people, with room for a further 5,000 standing. People were seated according to their status in Roman society – the more important you were, the nearer the killing you sat. Of course, the emperor had the best seat in the building, right at the front of one of the arena's long sides. His family, friends, and favourites sat nearby. Women, slaves, and the poor

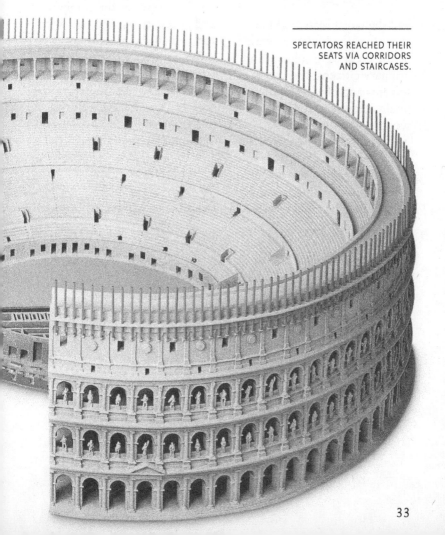

SPECTATORS REACHED THEIR SEATS VIA CORRIDORS AND STAIRCASES.

had the worst seats, right at the top of the building. Seated below them were soldiers and ordinary citizens, then civil servants and officers, and finally, closest to the ringside, senators and their guests.

With so many spectators crammed inside, crowd-control in the Colosseum was essential. The building was designed so that it could be emptied quickly and safely at the end of a show, with crowds spewing from its *vomitoria* (openings) onto the city streets. There were 80 of these entrance-and-exit places, of which the public could use 76. Two were for the emperor and his courtiers, and two were for gladiatorial processions.

On hot days a canopy was stretched across the arena to give shade for the spectators, so they could watch the suffering in the arena in comfort! This vast, billowing sun-blind,

THE FLOOR OF THE COLOSSEUM IS LONG GONE, SO TODAY'S VISITORS CAN SEE THE UNDERGROUND PASSAGES AND CHAMBERS.

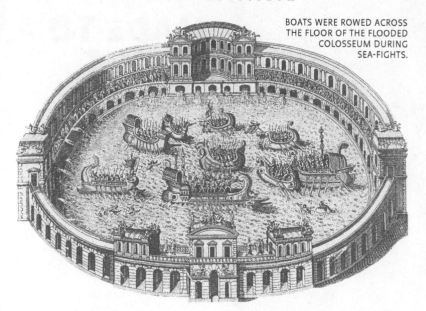

BOATS WERE ROWED ACROSS
THE FLOOR OF THE FLOODED
COLOSSEUM DURING
SEA-FIGHTS.

called the *velarium*, was operated by sailors. They were used to working with ships' ropes and canvas sails – the same materials that the *velarium* was made from.

Naval battles were so popular they were moved to a lake by the River Tiber. Then a network of passages was dug beneath the arena. In this

THE ENTIRE COLOSSEUM COULD BE EVACUATED IN THREE MINUTES.

Sea-fights in the city

When the Colosseum was first built, it was possible to flood the floor of the arena, because the ground beneath was solid and water did not leak away. If you'd been in the crowd at one of the early games, you might have seen a sea-fight, when gladiators fought on the decks of ships that floated on this artificial lake.

gloomy underworld, animals were kept in pens, ready to be sent up to their slaughter. Other parts of this hot, noisy labyrinth housed gladiators – the stars of the show who were about to have their moment of glory or disaster. For beasts and gladiators alike, there was no turning back. It was time to entertain the excited crowd, who were baying for blood!

35

MADE TO FIGHT

Gladiators were made, not born. Only the most unfortunate people became gladiators. They were sent to schools where they were given lessons in stabbing, slashing, and strangling. Pupils were taught a simple rule – do it to them before they do it to you!

IN ORDER TO BECOME A HERO OF THE ARENA, A GLADIATOR FIRST HAD TO LEARN THE ART OF KILLING.

Six gladiators and a funeral

In 264 BCE, there was a fight at a Roman funeral. It was the funeral of one of Rome's wealthy citizens, Decimus Junius Brutus Pera. The six men who fought in his honour were probably the first gladiators to perform in Rome. These fighters weren't performing just to entertain the living – they were also there to give thanks for the dead man's life. It was a way of keeping his memory

A TOMB CARVING OF GLADIATORS FROM ABOUT 30 BCE. IT MAY BE A SCENE FROM THE DEAD PERSON'S FUNERAL GAMES.

alive in the minds of the living, so that he wouldn't be forgotten.

At this time, some 350 years before the Colosseum was built, there were no arenas to fight in. Instead, the men who performed at this small show fought in the city's cattle market. No one who witnessed their contest could possibly have guessed that it marked the start of Rome's liking for blood-sports.

Spilling the blood

The idea of a fight at a funeral seems strange to our way of thinking. But it wasn't like this for the Romans. The Etruscans before them may have staged fights at funerals, in which a person was sacrificed. Perhaps the Romans liked the idea so much that they copied it. The main purpose of gladiatorial

games at funerals was to spill blood – it was a "gift" from the living to the dead. In their wills, wealthy or important Romans often asked for funeral games (*munera*) to be held in their honour. In staging the games, families paid respect to their dead relatives. Because funeral games were expensive, few

WEIRD WORLD

TO INSPIRE THEIR "STUDENTS", GLADIATOR TRAINERS TOLD STORIES OF BRAVE WARRIORS WHO HAD FOUGHT WELL, SURVIVED, AND ENDED UP OWNING GRAND HOUSES, SLAVES, AND EVEN THEIR OWN GLADIATORS.

families could afford them, so they became a way for the rich to show off their wealth in public.

Funeral games gradually grew in popularity in Rome. Records tell us that in 216 BCE, 22 pairs of gladiators fought at a funeral,

Roman life. The shows became bigger, bloodier, and more spectacular than ever.

Victims and volunteers
Gladiators were a commodity to be bought and sold, just like

A GLADIATOR HAD ABOUT THREE FIGHTS A YEAR – IF THEY SURVIVED!

and at a funeral in 183 BCE there were 60 pairs of fighters. As the games grew in size and became more exciting to watch, larger crowds turned up.

Some of the first gladiatorial contests were held in the Forum, the city's main square. With the opening of the Colosseum, in 80 CE, the crowds flocked to this purpose-built killing-ground. By then, gladiators were part of

cattle. The last thing anyone wanted was a shortage of gladiators. Fortunately, there was a constant supply of victims. Most of the gladiators were outcasts from society – prisoners-of-war, criminals, or slaves. These were people from the lowest level of society, who had no choice about their fate.

Can you believe that some Roman citizens volunteered to become gladiators? They were

THE RUINS OF ROME'S FORUM, WHERE THE FIRST GLADIATORS ONCE FOUGHT. WOODEN SEATING WAS PUT UP FOR THE SPECTATORS.

VERCINGETORIX, LEADER OF THE GAULS, SURRENDERS TO JULIUS CAESAR IN 52 BCE. THE ROMANS FORCED MANY PRISONERS OF WAR TO BECOME GLADIATORS.

unable to find work, or had lost their fortunes, and actually chose to become gladiators. They knew that they would be fed three times a day, have a place to sleep, receive money for every fight, and be given medical care for their injuries. But most of all, they knew that if they could survive long enough they would be free to return to their families – hopefully with enough money to start their lives over again. This much was good news.

The bad news was that volunteers had to swear an oath. They had to agree to be branded, shackled with chains, whipped with rods, pay for their food with their blood, and, if the worst happened, to be killed.

If you think it was only men who fought in the arena, think again. Emperor Domitian put on shows involving women. But a later emperor, Septimius Severus, banned any fights between women in 200 CE.

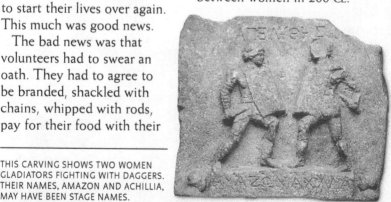

THIS CARVING SHOWS TWO WOMEN GLADIATORS FIGHTING WITH DAGGERS. THEIR NAMES, AMAZON AND ACHILLIA, MAY HAVE BEEN STAGE NAMES.

AT THIS FIGHTING SCHOOL IN POMPEII, GLADIATORS WERE TRAINED TO KILL BEFORE APPEARING IN THE TOWN'S ARENA.

He disapproved of women working as gladiators. The rest of Roman society, however, enjoyed their deadly duels.

Schools for gladiators

Some people made money out of gladiators. They were called *lanistae*, and became managers for groups of fighters, hiring them out for fights in return for money. Some *lanistae* became very wealthy doing this.

Gladiators were taught the craft of killing at special schools called *ludi*. They were large, well-run places, like army camps. The trainees lived in barracks and were usually only allowed out of the school when they had to appear in a contest. Discipline was strict, and those who broke the rules were punished by being sent to the school's prison.

Sick or injured fighters were no use to anyone, so trainee gladiators were well looked after. They were given plenty of boiled beans and stodgy barley to eat – foods that filled them up and made their muscles strong (gladiators were nicknamed *hordearii*, meaning "barley eaters"). Their health was just as important as their

bulging muscles. Injuries and illnesses were treated by the school's highly skilled doctors.

Teachers and techniques

Trainees were taught by older warriors who were once gladiators themselves. They had retired from the arena and gone on to work as teachers. All schools had a small arena where teachers taught their pupils how to fight. At first, new gladiators practised fighting against a tall wooden post, called a *palus*, which was rammed into the ground. The trainees were told to imagine the post was their enemy, and they attacked it with weapons chosen by their teacher. Sometimes they fought against a "man of straw" – a soft, squishy, body-shaped sack. Like the wooden post, it couldn't fight back.

IN THIS FILM SCENE, A TRAINER MARKS OUT TARGET ZONES ON THE BODY OF SPARTACUS, SO OPPONENTS WILL KNOW WHERE TO AIM.

WEIRD WORLD

IN 73 BCE, SPARTACUS, A SLAVE WHO WAS A GLADIATOR, LED A REBELLION AGAINST ROME. IT TOOK 10 ROMAN LEGIONS TO DEFEAT HIM. ABOUT 6,000 OF SPARTACUS'S FOLLOWERS WERE CRUCIFIED.

The trainees learned how to fight by using wooden swords and other blunt weapons. It was far too risky to let them use real weapons until they could be trusted with them – just in case they used them against their teachers and escaped from the school, or tried to commit suicide. Only after lots of training were they allowed to practise against other gladiators.

The fighters who trained and lived together at a gladiatorial school got to know each other very well, and they probably became friends. They were known as a *familia gladiatoria* ("family of gladiators"). The fights they had were pretend, and no one really got hurt. But, when it was time to entertain the crowd and fight for real, the gladiators knew they might end up killing their friends…

INTO THE ARENA

You are a trained gladiator at the peak of physical fitness. The day of the games is almost here, and you are soon to enter the arena. But how will you fight? Who will you fight, and what weapons will you use? Will you live to see another day? We can only guess what went through the minds of Rome's brave gladiators as they prepared for their few minutes of fame.

THIS STATUETTE SHOWS A *THRAEX* GLADIATOR WEARING LEG PROTECTORS, A CRESTED HELMET, AND AN ARM GUARD.

The show comes to town
Gladiatorial shows were provided for free to the public, and only the wealthiest Romans could afford to put them on. Shows were advertised days before a troupe of gladiators reached town. Painted signs appeared on the walls and the excitement of the public grew. Town criers walked the streets calling out the fighters' names and skills, and people carried banners broadcasting the same news. Get-rich-quick merchants set up souvenir stalls close to the arena, selling gladiator goodies – from pottery models of gladiators to decorated oil lamps. This build-up ensured that the amphitheatre would be packed on the big day.

One last supper

Gladiators came to town the day before the games began. They were guests of the wealthy patron (known as the *editor*) who was giving the show. That night, at a grand banquet held in the fighters' honour, the public watched them eat. It was a chance to "eye up" the gladiators and decide who looked like they'd fight well, and who wouldn't. The gladiators knew that this might be the last food they'd ever eat. Some made the most of it and stuffed their faces – can you blame them? A few couldn't stomach the food and spent the evening pleading with members of the public to take messages to their families.

GAMES BEGAN WITH ANIMAL FIGHTS. THIS FIGHTER FACES A LION AND A LEOPARD.

43

A REFEREE ENSURES THAT TWO
GLADIATORS KEEP TO THE RULES
IN THIS MOSAIC SCENE.

across the sandy floor, followed
by slaves carrying their arms
and armour. The crowd of
50,000 spectators roared
with delight. When the
gladiators came to a
halt in front of the
emperor's platform,
however, the cheering
stopped. Raising their
right hands towards the
emperor, the gladiators
chanted these famous
Latin words, *"Ave,
Imperator, morituri te
salutant!"* ("Hail,
Emperor, those who are
about to die salute thee!").

Gladiators in action

Games held at the Colosseum
followed a set pattern. The day
started with animal hunts, held
in the morning. The mood
changed at midday when
criminals were executed. This
was a foretaste for the highlight
of the day – the gladiatorial
contests held in the afternoon.
At a large event there could be
hundreds of gladiators in action.
Smaller shows made do with
fewer fighters, a typical number
being about 30.

Dressed in purple cloaks
embroidered in gold, the
fighters walked through
the Colosseum's gladiatorial
entrances. Once inside the
great building they marched

Know your enemy

In full view of the crowd, so
that no one could be accused
of cheating, the gladiators
found out who they were to
fight. The holder of the games
and the gladiators' teachers
decided how the warriors were
to be paired, one against one.
They usually matched fighters
of equal ability against each
other. A gladiator who had
survived five fights might be
paired against an opponent
of the same rank. Mass fights
between whole troops of
gladiators were held only
at the largest games.

The contest began with
warm-up fights. No one got
badly hurt, since only blunt

wooden weapons were used. Their purpose was to get the gladiators in the fighting spirit, and to excite the crowd.

There were at least 16 (maybe as many as 20) different types of gladiator. A fighter was trained as one particular type, ranging from a lightly armed *secutor* ("chaser") or *retiarius* ("net-fighter") to a more heavily armed *thraex* ("Thracian") and *murmillo* (named after the fish emblem on his helmet). Each type was instantly recognizable by the crowd, and spectators knew how each type of gladiator would fight.

At a sign from the holder of the games, the band began to play. Musicians sounded trumpets, flutes, horns, and wheezy water organs, and amid this noise the fighting began.

MAXIMUS (RIGHT), THE HERO OF THE SMASH-HIT FILM *GLADIATOR*, FIGHTS FOR HIS LIFE IN THE ARENA.

THE SHRILL SOUND OF TRUMPETS ADDED DRAMA TO THE CONTEST.

Who fought who

Several pairs of gladiators fought at the same time, with certain types often matched against each other. For example, a *murmillo* often fought a *thraex*. The *murmillo* was armed with a short sword called a *gladius* (from which we get the word "gladiator"). This type of gladiator carried a tall, rectangular wooden shield, and was protected by head, arm, and leg armour. A *thraex* carried a smaller shield and fought with a short, curved sword. The *thraex* too was protected by armour, but the torsos of both types of gladiators were left bare, providing visible flesh for an opponent to strike at.

The *retiarus's* usual opponent was the *secutor*. The *secutor* had a specially designed helmet that was round and smooth so that it wouldn't get caught in the *retiarus's* net. It had two small eye holes to protect the *secutor's* eyes from the *retiarus's* trident.

Rules are rules

Movies often give the impression that gladiators fought in a frenzy, exchanging wild blows with each other. They didn't. The truth is that gladiator duels were skillful fights with strict rules to follow. Unfortunately, we don't know much about the rules. What we do know is that referees had the power to halt a fight. For instance, if a piece of armour fell off, the referees could stop the fight while the gladiator put it back on – and then the fight continued.

Delivering the knock-out blow

If the gladiators were not fighting hard enough, referees sent attendants called *lorarii* (named after their *"lora"* or leather straps) to thrash the fighters. It was all part of the entertainment, and the crowd loved it. As blood began to flow, the cheering increased. And when a gladiator fell to the floor, the crowd knew the fatal blow could soon be on its way.

Fallen gladiators had one chance for survival. As they lay on their backs, they raised their left hands to appeal for mercy. If they

had fought well, the crowd might want them to live. People waved their handkerchiefs, raised their thumbs, and called out, *"Mitte!"* ("Let them go!"). Then all eyes turned to see whether the giver of the games would agree. If they did, the gladiator was pardoned... but next time might not be so lucky.

If the crowd thought the gladiator had put on a poor performance, they showed no mercy. As their thumbs turned down and cries of *"Iugula!"* ("Kill him!") rang across the arena, the

WEIRD WORLD
GLADIATORS WERE ADVERTISED BY THEIR "STAGE NAMES", SUCH AS PUGNAX ("QUARRELSOME ONE"), TIGRIS ("TIGER"), OR COLUMBUS ("DOVE"). FANS LOOKED FORWARD TO SEEING THE STAR FIGHTERS IN ACTION.

victim knew they were about to meet their end. Again, the games' sponsor had the last word. If they turned their thumb down, it was the signal for the doomed fighter to "take the iron" and be finished off. Their opponent executed them where they lay, and the people shouted, *"Habet!"* ("That's got them!").

IN THE FILM *SPARTACUS*, THE REBEL GLADIATOR (RIGHT), ARMED AS A THRACIAN, GRAPPLES WITH A NET-FIGHTER.

Thumbs up or thumbs down?

Here's a puzzle that continues to baffle historians. No one can be totally certain if "thumbs down" really was the sign of the death sentence. Some experts think we've got it dead wrong. They say "thumbs down" meant "put the sword away", as if sliding it back into its scabbard, whereas "thumbs up" meant "stick it in them". The fact is, we just don't know. The prevailing view seems to be that the Romans used the "thumbs down" gesture when they wanted a fighter to die – which just shows how easy it is to believe so-called "facts" which might, in fact, turn out to be fiction!

A *THRAEX* STABS AT A *MURMILLO*'S NECK WITH HIS CURVED SWORD. MOST GLADIATORS WHO DIED IN THE ARENA WERE AGED BETWEEN 18 AND 25.

WINNING GLADIATORS DID A LAP OF HONOUR AROUND THE ARENA, WEARING LAUREL WREATHS AND WAVING PALM BRANCHES IN THE AIR.

Winners and losers

By the end of a contest, the floor of the arena was drenched in blood.

The sand was raked over and dead gladiators were taken away on stretchers to the mortuary, where their throats were cut. Why? To make sure they really astonishing 4 times. But he never took the chance to retire. This may seem odd to us, but fighting was all that many gladiators knew.

IN EIGHT GAMES, AUGUSTUS SENT 10,000 FIGHTERS INTO THE ARENA.

were dead, and not trying to fake their own deaths! As for the wounded, they were patched up by doctors who made sure they would live to fight again.

And the victorious winners? These gladiators had become the new heroes of the arena. They were presented with their winnings – money and a palm branch. For excellent results, the best fighters were given a laurel wreath to wear on their heads.

The greatest prize of all was the *rudis* – a wooden sword. It was a sign that a gladiator had been given his freedom and could retire to enjoy the money and fame he had earned. One gladiator, named Flamma, seems to have had a remarkable career. He fought 34 times, won 21, drew 9, and was "let go" an

Those who did retire often returned to their gladiator schools to teach the next generation of fighters the brutal skills they needed to stay alive in the arena.

A GLADIATOR RAISES HIS SWORD IN TRIUMPH OVER HIS SLAIN OPPONENT.

HUNTERS AND CHARIOTEERS

The people of Rome had lots of time off work. By the 3rd century CE, they enjoyed 200 public holidays a year! The city's authorities knew that if the people had nothing to do in their spare time, they might get bored and start rioting. As well as gladiatorial games, the state organized other entertainment to try to keep the masses happy – and it worked.

GIRAFFES WERE JUST ONE OF THE EXOTIC ANIMALS BROUGHT TO ROME.

Animals to the slaughter

Gladiators were not the only creatures to die in the arena. Games held at the Colosseum usually combined the killing of men – and sometimes women – with the mass slaughter of animals. The general rule was that animals were slaughtered in the morning, while humans were bumped off at lunchtime and in the afternoon.

The Romans had a word for shows that featured animals – *venationes*. Strictly speaking, this word means "animal hunts", but the shows weren't always as savage as it suggests. At some events, animals were paraded before the crowd simply because they were unusual species seldom seen in Rome. Imagine being there when a giraffe went on show. People were amazed that such an odd-looking animal could exist. The Roman name for a giraffe was "spotted camel" (*camelopardalis*).

Other shows were more like present-day circus acts, where dangerous animals performed at elephants, elephants gored rhinoceroses, and so on. At other times, archers shot arrows at animals from the safety of metal cages – this way there was little danger of them ending up as animal food.

Massacre in the arena

The highlight of an animal show was when the animal fighters, the *venatores*, and their assistants, the *bestiarii*, entered the arena. Just like gladiators, animal fighters were condemned criminals, prisoners-of-war, and volunteers, and they received a similar sort of training. Despite their similarity to gladiators, the public regarded animal fighters as inferior beings.

tricks – perhaps a tiger licking the hand of its trainer, a team of panthers pulling chariots, or an elephant dancing and walking a tightrope. The crowd thought it was great fun, but killing was what they were really there for – and they soon got it. Some animal shows were little more than blood-fests, with wild animals savaging each other to death. Bears fought bulls, bulls charged

AN ENRAGED BULL AND A FEROCIOUS BEAR FIGHT TO THE DEATH, TORMENTED BY A BESTIARIUS WITH A LONG HOOK.

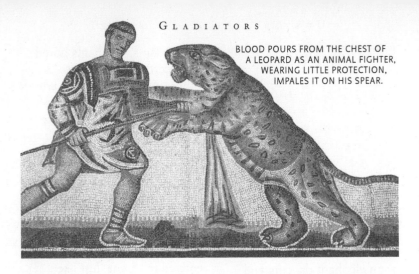

BLOOD POURS FROM THE CHEST OF A LEOPARD AS AN ANIMAL FIGHTER, WEARING LITTLE PROTECTION, IMPALES IT ON HIS SPEAR.

Wearing little more than tunics and leg-wrappings, and armed only with long spears, animal-fighters hunted a variety of animals, from harmless hares to human-eating lions. The *venatores* stalked them on foot, or chased them on horseback.

32 elephants, 10 elks, 10 tigers, 60 tame lions, 10 wild lions, 30 leopards, 10 hyenas, 10 camels, 20 wild asses (perhaps zebras), 40 wild horses, 6 hippos, and a rhinoceros. All the animals were either killed or displayed to the crowd.

TRAINED ELEPHANTS WROTE IN THE SAND WITH THEIR TRUNKS.

The *bestiarii* were on standby to whip the animals into a rage, making the show even more cruel than it already was.

Some idea of the different types of animal seen in the Colosseum comes from a show organized by Emperor Philip the Arab in 247 CE to celebrate the 1,000th birthday of Rome. Records show that there were

Virtual reality hunts
But why were the Romans so cruel to animals? Well, you might think they were cruel, but most Romans didn't think like this. Hunting animals was a favourite Roman blood-sport, and watching a hunt in the arena was a reminder of this. Most people who lived in Rome never left the city, so

they had little chance of going on a real hunt in the nearby fields and forests. For these city dwellers, a show in the arena was their equivalent of "virtual reality", where the countryside appeared before their eyes, complete with wild animals, scenery, trees… and hunters.

Animals were transported to Rome from all over the empire. Africa supplied lions, leopards, monkeys, crocodiles, hippos, rhinos, and ostriches. Elephants travelled from Africa and Asia, and wild boars came from the forests of northern Europe. At the Colosseum, animals were kept in rooms and cages under the floor of the arena. Lifts raised them to the surface where they appeared, as if by magic, through trapdoors.

Thrown to the beasts

The Romans learned many things from their friends and enemies – and not all of them were pleasant! For example, they got the idea of throwing criminals to wild beasts from the Carthaginians of North Africa, who used elephants to squash army deserters to death.

In Roman hands, this method of execution became a gory spectacle. Men and women who had committed serious crimes were tied to wooden posts in the arena, where lions,

THOUSANDS OF WILD ANIMALS WERE CAPTURED AND TAKEN TO ROME FOR THE HUNTS. MANY CAME BY SHIP FROM AFRICA.

IN THIS MOSAIC OF AN ANIMAL SHOW, A MAN SENTENCED TO BE KILLED BY WILD ANIMALS IS WHEELED TO HIS DEATH. ANOTHER MAN IS ATTACKED TO HIS LEFT.

leopards, and tigers ripped them to shreds. It was a slow, painful death. These executions took place at lunchtime, and some Romans were sickened by the sight – it was enough to turn their stomachs!

A visit to the race-track

Another favourite Roman spectator sport was chariot-racing. Just as the Colosseum was the biggest arena in the Roman world, the Circus Maximus ("Greatest Circus"), also in Rome, was the largest of all circuses, or race-tracks. Measuring 600 m (1,970 ft) long and 80 m (260 ft) wide, the track formed a long, narrow rectangle with rounded ends. With room for about 200,000 spectators, the Circus Maximus was four times larger than the Colosseum and bigger than any of today's super-stadiums!

Charioteers were thought of as low-class people, just as gladiators and animal-fighters

A CHARIOTEER OF THE VENETI, OR BLUE TEAM, STANDS BY HIS HORSE.

were. They, too, were usually slaves, or former slaves who had been granted their freedom. Some became rich and famous because they won many races, such as Pompeius Musclosus, who had 3,559 victories! The

charioteers belonged to different racing clubs (*factiones* or factions), which were cheered on by fans, just as sports teams are today. There were only four clubs, and the charioteers wore the colours of their team. The *Albati* team wore white, the *Russati* wore red, the *Prasini* was the green team, and blue was the colour of the *Veneti*.

CHARIOTS RACED AROUND A LONG PLINTH IN THE MIDDLE OF THE CIRCUS MAXIMUS.

55

The different colours made it easy for the crowd to work out who was who as the chariots charged around the track.

The horses came from Spain, Greece, and North Africa, and some became as well-known as the charioteers themselves. By today's standards, Roman horses were larger than a pony, but smaller than a full-sized modern horse. Horses usually pulled chariots in teams of two or four, harnessed side by side, but sometimes up to 10 were used.

On your marks, get set, go!
A race meeting began with a parade. It was a chance for the public to view the charioteers and bet on who they thought would win. On a signal from the race starter, the gates of

the starting boxes were flung open and the chariots thundered out. At the Circus Maximus, up to 12 chariots raced at a time, driving anti-clockwise around the track for seven laps. They covered 5.2 km (3.2 miles), reaching speeds of up to 75 km/h (46 mph). Races probably lasted between 8 and 9 minutes.

WEIRD WORLD
CURSES, WRITTEN ON PIECES OF LEAD, WERE SOMETIMES BURIED OUTSIDE THE RACE-TRACK BY PEOPLE WHO WANTED A PARTICULAR CHARIOTEER TO HAVE AN ACCIDENT, SO THAT THEIR OWN FAVOURITE WOULD WIN!

Dangers of the track
Charioteers needed all their skills, not only to control their horses but also to avoid crashing into the other chariots. But pile-ups did happen, especially at each end of the track, where there was a sharp turn. And it wasn't just the charioteers and their horses who risked their lives. Boys stood at the edge of the race-track throwing water to refresh the horses and drivers – careless lads ended up under the chariot wheels.

The biggest race meetings at the Circus Maximus usually had 24 races a day, involving about 1,000 horses. In between races, acrobats kept the noisy crowd entertained, racing at full speed as they jumped from one horse to the next. At the end of a meeting, the winners received the same sort of prizes as victorious gladiators did – palm branches and lots of money.

THE FILM *BEN HUR* RECREATED A CHARIOT RACE AT THE CIRCUS MAXIMUS.

EVERYDAY LIFE

You've probably seen the Colosseum on TV. You may even have visited a place where Romans lived – a town, a villa, or maybe a fort. It's difficult to imagine that jumbles of broken walls were once buildings, but to the Romans they were homes and places of work. So what was it like to live in a Roman city? What did people do, what did they eat, and what clothes did they wear?

WOMEN WORE EARRINGS AND NECKLACES. THEIR HAIR WAS TIED BACK AND HELD IN PLACE WITH PINS AND RIBBONS.

Costume customs

Clothes were usually made from wool or linen. The basic item of clothing worn by absolutely everyone – men, women, and children – was the tunic (*tunica*). This simple, loose garment hung from the shoulders to just below the knees, like a long shirt. It could be worn with or without sleeves, and was fastened at the waist by a belt. Tunics were either plain or decorated on the front and back with vertical coloured stripes (*clavi*).

Men and women also wore the same types of shoes. Leather sandals and slippers (*socci*) were worn indoors, while boots were worn outdoors. Peasants and slaves wore clogs with hard-wearing wooden soles.

What did Romans wear under their tunics? That's an extremely personal question! If you must know, men and women wore a loincloth (*subligaculum*). It was a loose-fitting cloth worn around the hips like a kilt. (This was the only thing that gladiators wore under their armour!) Women

wore tight linen or leather bands around their chests. They were the equivalent of corsets, but some wore them over their tunics rather than underneath.

Heavyweight garment
Over the tunic, male Roman citizens wore a heavy robe called a *toga*. Its name probably comes from the Latin word *tegere*, meaning "to cover" – which is exactly what it did. Made from a single piece of fabric, semi-circular in shape, the *toga* was large enough to cover the man

WEIRD WORLD
LIKE US, THE ROMANS COULD BE VERY VAIN. BALD MEN GREW THEIR HAIR LONG ON ONE SIDE AND COMBED IT OVER THEIR HEADS, WHILE SPOTTY PEOPLE STUCK CLOTH PATCHES OVER THEIR PIMPLES.

THESE WOMEN ARE IN THEIR OUTDOOR CLOTHES. EACH WOMAN HAS A SHAWL DRAPED OVER HER *STOLA*.

PALLA

STOLA

SANDALS

from head to toe. It was so big that a man usually needed someone to help him drape it around his body in the correct way. Like the tunic, the *toga* could be decorated with bands of colour. It was mainly worn on formal occasions, particularly by officials. Workers and slaves wore simpler clothes.

Slip into a *stola*

The *stola* was the standard item of outer clothing for women. It was a long gown worn with a chest belt that caused it to hang down in folds. Some gowns had

sleeves, some didn't – it was a matter of taste. Over her *stola* (especially if she was outside) a woman wore a *palla*, which was a long shawl. She might also wear a scarf, tied at her neck.

Father of the family

In Roman society, a "family" meant much more than a mother, a father, and their children. It also included the wives of the family's sons, and their children too. For much of Roman history, the oldest living male – the *paterfamilias* – was the head of the family. It was his duty to provide for the family and educate the children.

When a child was born into a Roman family, the father had a choice to make – whether to recognize it as his, or not. If he took the baby in his arms, it was the sign of welcome into his family. If he did not pick the child up, it showed that he

WEIRD WORLD

THE ROMAN WRITER PLINY THE ELDER (23–79 CE) RECOMMENDED THAT SPIDERS' WEBS BE APPLIED TO CUTS FROM SHAVING TO STOP THE BLEEDING!

wanted nothing to do with it, and the infant was left outside to die. The infant's one and only chance of survival was if a stranger found it, in which case the child would be brought up as a slave.

Child-killing seems so cruel today. But a new baby was another mouth to feed. If the child was born to a poor family, where the father couldn't provide any more food, it's not difficult to see why he might choose to let it die.

By 374 CE, under the rule of Emperor Valentinian, a father's right of life or death over his children had more or less come to an end. From then on, a father who committed such a terrible act was guilty of murder.

Naming baby

Boys were named nine days after they were born, and girls when they were eight days old. At a naming ceremony, prayers were said and a male baby was given a round lucky charm (*bulla*) to wear around his neck, and a baby girl was given a crescent-moon shaped amulet called a *lunula*. A boy wore his *bulla* until his 16th birthday. Only then could he remove it to show that he had become an adult.

Women and marriage

A girl removed her *lunula* on the eve of her wedding day – usually when she was 14 or 15. That was the day she was "placed in the hands," as the Romans said, of her husband. From then on, she was his responsibility, not her father's. Boys were allowed to marry from the age of 14, although most married in their late teens or early twenties.

Most marriages were arranged between the heads of the two families involved. A girl might not even know the name of her husband-to-be until after her

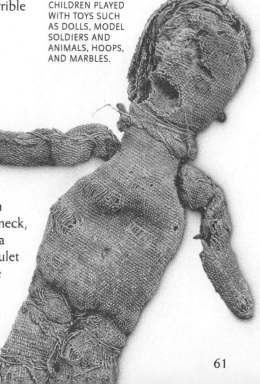

CHILDREN PLAYED WITH TOYS SUCH AS DOLLS, MODEL SOLDIERS AND ANIMALS, HOOPS, AND MARBLES.

61

IN THIS STONE CARVING, A COUPLE HOLD HANDS AND EXCHANGE VOWS AT THEIR WEDDING. THE GROOM HOLDS THE MARRIAGE CONTRACT IN HIS HAND.

father had decided who she was going to marry! An engagement party was held at which the girl was given a betrothal ring by her fiancé, and he received a dowry (a gift of money) from her father. June was thought to be the best time to hold a wedding, since it was the month of the goddess Juno, whose duty it was to protect marriages. At the ceremony, the couple signed a contract to pledge themselves to each other, prayers were said, and sacrifices were offered to the gods. After enjoying a feast of food and wine, the couple went to live in the groom's house.

Traditional Romans believed that a woman's place was in the home, running the household, spinning and weaving wool, giving orders to slaves, and caring for children. Even Roman empresses wove wool. Despite this, many women had their own businesses, and they played an important public role as priestesses.

Home sweet home

Roman town houses were of two types – private ones for the wealthy, and apartments for the poor. However, if you were very rich, you might have owned a big house in the countryside. This was a villa – a place to escape to at weekends, far from the noise and dirt of the town.

A town house (*domus*) was a one or two-storey building lived in by a family and its servants. Unlike a modern house, the *domus* only had a few small windows on the outside. Roman houses were designed to look in on themselves, not out. They were built around two open spaces: a hallway (*atrium*) and a garden (*peristylium*). The bedrooms, kitchen, dining rooms, servants' quarters, and storerooms were all arranged around the hallway and garden. Heating was provided by coal burning in metal braziers,

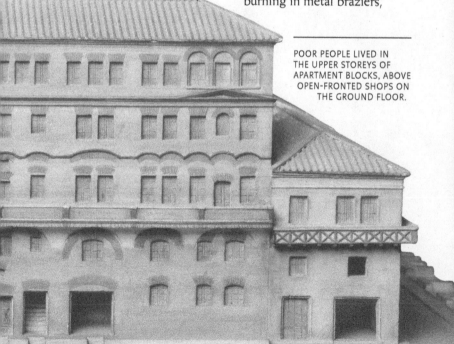

POOR PEOPLE LIVED IN THE UPPER STOREYS OF APARTMENT BLOCKS, ABOVE OPEN-FRONTED SHOPS ON THE GROUND FLOOR.

which could be moved from room to room. The house was private, with no danger of being overlooked by nosey neighbours.

If you weren't so wealthy and lived in an apartment block, you would have got to know your neighbours very well. Never mind about waving at them from your window, you could have leaned out and touched them! Rome's apartment blocks, up to five storeys tall, housed the city's poor in cramped conditions. The rooms were small and dark, cold, and dirty. There was no running water, no heating, and no toilets – guess what went out of the window! To brighten up their squalid surroundings, some people grew flowers in window boxes.

A BANQUET WITH MANY COURSES TOOK SEVERAL HOURS TO EAT. PEOPLE ATE WITH THEIR FINGERS, OR WITH KNIVES AND SPOONS – THE ROMANS DIDN'T USE FORKS.

What's on the menu?

At dawn, after a good night's sleep in your comfortable town house, or a restless one if your

MANY POORER PEOPLE BOUGHT FOOD FROM "TAKE-AWAY" SHOPS LIKE THIS ONE IN POMPEII. HOT AND COLD FOOD WAS SERVED FROM POTTERY JARS SUNK INTO THE TOPS OF COUNTERS.

noisy neighbours had kept you awake in your apartment, it was time to rise and shine and get dressed. Before the day's work began, there was just enough time to grab a cup of water and a mouthful of food for the first meal of the day, usually something cold from the previous night. The midday meal was much the same – more of yesterday's leftovers, or a piece of bread and some fruit. It was really just a snack.

The main meal of the day was dinner (*cena*). For the rich, this was a feast that might start at three in the afternoon and go on to late at night. It was eaten, after the daily bath, in the dining-room (*triclinium*). On three sides of the room were low couches where the family and their guests reclined, lying on their left sides. In the middle was a table, on which the food was placed – and lots of it. Some banquets had separate courses of fish, snails, meat, vegetables, birds, fruit, nuts, and pastries. Adults drank plenty of wine too.

Time for a bath

People didn't bother to wash when they woke up, since they knew they'd be having a bath later in the day – and what a bath it was! Only the poshest of houses had bathrooms, so most people cleaned up

65

THE ROMAN BATHS AT THE TOWN OF AQUAE SULIS (BATH) IN ENGLAND.

at the public baths (*thermae*). Town baths were usually large buildings – the baths built in Rome by Emperor Caracalla had room for 1,600 visitors at a time!

Men and women bathed at different times in small bath houses and had separate areas in large public baths. Mixed bathing was not allowed. The layout of bath houses suggest that Romans moved from cold to progressively hotter rooms, gradually acclimatizing their bodies. However, many bathers did not follow this plan. Some people would begin by exercising to work up a sweat, others would have a cold plunge bath.

Taking a bath was a social occasion too – a chance to chat, gossip, and catch up on the news.

Water supply

Roman cities needed vast amounts of water for bathing, drinking, and washing waste away from their lavatories. Much of this was supplied by aqueducts. These were waterways that channelled water from rivers, lakes, and springs to built-up areas,

THE CONTAINER ABOVE HELD OIL, WHICH WAS SPRINKLED ON A PERSON'S SKIN. A METAL SCRAPER CALLED A STRIGIL (ABOVE LEFT) WAS USED TO REMOVE IT.

using tunnels and huge stone bridges to overcome hills, valleys, and any other obstacles that stood in their way.

mourners (whose job was to wail and cry) walked slowly in a funeral procession towards a cemetery outside the town. At

ROASTED DORMICE, DIPPED IN HONEY, WERE A FAVOURITE ROMAN SNACK.

Health, death, and burial
Romans suffered from the same diseases and illnesses as we do, but their life expectancy was shorter. Only the wealthy, who ate good food and could afford doctors and medical treatment, were more likely to live past their 60th birthday. The poor were lucky to reach their 40s or 50s. After they died, people were usually buried rather than cremated. Relatives, flute-players, and professional

a rich person's funeral, relatives wore masks to represent the dead person's ancestors – it was a way of bringing the family together. The Romans believed that the spirit lived on after death, but they only had vague ideas of what the afterlife was like.

THE PONT DU GARD, SOUTHERN FRANCE, WAS BOTH AN AQUEDUCT (TOP LEVEL) AND A ROAD BRIDGE (BOTTOM LEVEL).

THE ARTS OF ROME

Every civilization has its artistic side, and the Romans certainly had theirs. There was so much more to Roman life than trips to the savage arena and the thrills and spills race-track. Romans prided themselves on being educated, artistic, and cultured people. To them, it was everyone else who was brutal and barbaric.

Getting an education

There were no laws that said children had to go to school, and many, especially the children of poor people, had no schooling at all. Education was entirely the responsibility of one's parents. So, if someone grew up not knowing how to read, write, or count, they could blame it on parents!

Girls were usually educated at home, where they learned to read, write, spin, weave, keep accounts, and sometimes play musical instruments. Boys from the posh part of town were privately educated at home by personal teachers, who were usually slaves or former slaves. Most other boys were sent to schools, if their parents could afford it. Schools consisted of

A TEACHER GIVES A LESSON TO A GROUP OF PUPILS.

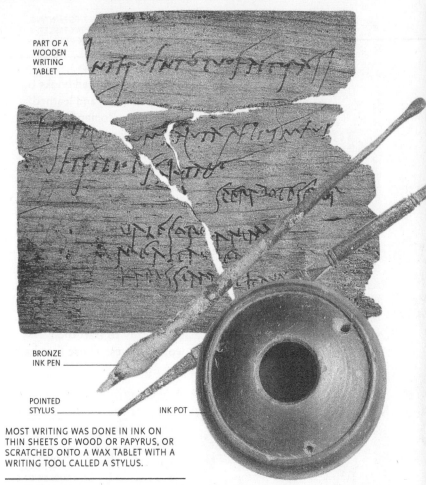

PART OF A WOODEN WRITING TABLET

BRONZE INK PEN

POINTED STYLUS

INK POT

MOST WRITING WAS DONE IN INK ON THIN SHEETS OF WOOD OR PAPYRUS, OR SCRATCHED ONTO A WAX TABLET WITH A WRITING TOOL CALLED A STYLUS.

a room hired by a teacher at the back of a shop, with just a curtain to separate the shoppers from the scholars.

School days

Boys usually began school at the age of seven. In Rome, the school day started early, usually just after dawn. Primary school children sat on wooden stools facing the teacher, who was perched in a high chair. Known as a *litterator*, the teacher taught the students how to read and write letters, as well as how to do simple sums. Children learned by copying and reciting letters, sentences, and numbers over and over again. At age 10 or 11, some boys from rich families went to grammar school.

69

THE ROMAN WOMAN IN THIS PAINTING HOLDS A STYLUS AND A WAX TABLET. THE MAN CLASPS A BOOK ROLL.

Latin language, read books by famous authors, and learned Greek – the Roman Empire's second language.

From the age of 14 or 15, a few boys were taught by a *rhetor*, who had a proper schoolroom, and was paid by the state to teach boys oratory (public speaking). Pupils learned how to speak fluently, ordering their thoughts clearly and choosing their words carefully. By the age of 20, these young men were ready to start their working lives. Those that had

Girls stopped their studies by this age and stayed at home until they got married. The grammar school teacher was a *grammaticus*. Boys attended this school, also behind a shop, for up to five years. They learned the rules (grammar) that governed the

THE LIBRARY OF CELSUS AT THE ROMAN CITY OF EPHESUS, TURKEY, ONCE HELD 12,000 BOOKS.

A ROMAN THEATRE RESEMBLED AN
ARENA WITH THE END CHOPPED OFF.

mastered oratory often worked
in the law or in politics, where
public speaking was important.

Books and libraries
A good education meant you'd
be able to read books and poems
by Roman and Greek writers.
Most Roman books weren't like
this one, with pages you can
turn. They were written by hand
(the Romans didn't know about
printing) on sheets of paper
made from the Egyptian papyrus
plant. Black and red ink was
used. Mistakes could be rubbed
out with a damp sponge. The

finished sheets were glued
together into rolls, each of about
20 sheets, then wrapped around
a winding stick (*umbilicus*). These
scrolls (book rolls) were stored
on their sides in the bookcases
of a library (*bibliotheca*). Finally,
labels were attached to the
scrolls to give their titles.

Watching a play
A visit to the theatre was a
popular pastime in towns and
cities throughout the empire.
Roman theatres didn't put on
performances whenever they
felt like it, as theatres do today.
Plays, like chariot races and
gladiator fights, were staged
on public holidays. But Roman

71

officials were eager to offer the people a wide range of events to choose from – blood and guts at the arena, or laughs and hisses at the theatre!

At first sight, a theatre, such as Rome's 12,000-seat Theatre of Marcellus, looks like half an arena. But the way you should really see it is the other way around – an arena is like two theatres joined together to make a circular (or oval) building. This is why an arena is known as an amphitheatre, which means "double-theatre".

Playing for laughs

Plays were performed in the afternoons, at the same time that gladiators were hacking lumps off each other in the arena. While theatre-goers were booing a bad actor, or pelting him with apples (never tomatoes, which didn't exist in Europe until the 1500s), people at the games might be sentencing a gladiator to death!

Mind you, Roman theatres enjoyed their share of side-splitting, too – laughter that is. People loved to see a rib-tickling comedy. Audiences showed their appreciation for well-performed plays by snapping their fingers, clapping, and, if it was really good, waving handkerchiefs and corners of their clothes. Serious plays, called tragedies, were just as popular, but without the laughs (maybe a few tears).

ACTORS WORE MASKS THAT LET THE AUDIENCE KNOW WHETHER THE PLAY WAS A TRAGEDY OR A COMEDY. THIS MASK WAS WORN IN A COMEDY.

A WALL PAINTING OF A RIOT IN 59 CE AT POMPEII'S ARENA. THE SUN-BLIND, OR CANOPY, IS AT THE TOP OF THE PICTURE.

Pictures in paint

The Romans were expert craft-workers. They excelled in decorating the walls, floors, and ceilings of their public and private buildings with pictures. Paintings were often designed to suit the function of the room in which they appeared. For example, pictures of fish and river scenes appeared in the baths, and the dining-rooms of houses featured hunting images, dead animals, and banquets.

Artists painted rooms with panels and bands of bright colour, particularly red. Some walls were decorated with landscape scenes, flowers, or figures from Greek and Roman mythology. To our eyes, these brightly coloured rooms can seem "over-the-top", but to the Romans they were the height of fashion and good taste.

We're lucky that any of these fragile paintings have survived at all, but many have. Some are documentary images, recording scenes from real life, just as newspaper photographs do today. An instance of this can be seen in a wall painting from Pompeii, a small town south of Rome, where an unknown artist painted a riot scene. The riot happened in 59 CE, in and

WEIRD WORLD

ROMAN ACTORS WERE SKILLED AT MAKING SOUND EFFECTS. FOR EXAMPLE, THE SOUND OF THUNDER WAS MADE BY ROLLING BRONZE BALLS DOWN A METAL TUBE SO THAT THEY CRASHED ONTO A SHEET OF TIN.

MOSAICS OFTEN PORTRAYED SCENES AND OBJECTS FROM EVERYDAY LIFE.

around the town's arena. The painting not only shows us the fight between the Pompeiians and visitors from Nuceria, but it also shows the arena's seats, stairways, entrances, and canopy.

Craft of the mosaic maker

If there's one Roman craft that everyone's heard of, it's mosaic – the art of making pictures from small cubes of coloured stone, glass, or pottery. But did you know that mosaic was actually invented by the Greeks, not the Romans? It's another example of how the Romans copied other people's good ideas. However, in the hands of the Roman mosaicists (that's the name for people who make mosaics), the craft reached perfection. The mosaics were made by laying different-coloured stone cubes, some just 5 mm (0.2 in) across, in wet plaster.

Mosaics were mainly used on floors, but some walls were also decorated with mosaic pictures. Like paintings, there was a range of mosaic styles to suit a person's taste and budget. The cheapest mosaics were simple

Glassware and pottery
The Romans were also skilled glassworkers. Flasks and bottles were mass-produced by blowing glass into moulds. Fine glassware might have bands of gold running through it.

ONE HOUSE IN POMPEII HAD A "BEWARE OF THE DOG" MOSAIC.

geometric patterns – squares, triangles, or diamonds – often made from large, roughly shaped cubes, or even pebbles. These patterns could be repeated over and over again until the whole floor was covered. More costly mosaics used tiny cubes to make highly detailed, life-like images of people, gods, and animals. Cubes of pure gold, rock-crystal, and rare marble were used in the most luxurious mosaics, giving them a stunning, jewel-like quality.

Potters were kept busy making all manner of ceramic vessels, from clay lamps, bowls, and cups to large storage vessels (*amphorae*) used to hold wine and oil. Pottery was often decorated with moulded pictures or, sometimes, given a glaze, which gave its surface a shiny, glass-like look. Many of the images on pots and in mosaics and paintings were of gods, goddesses, and scenes from the Roman religion, which was at the heart of Roman life.

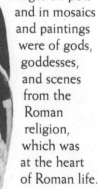

THIS BEAUTIFUL ROMAN VASE WAS MADE FROM COLOURED GLASS.

GODS AND TEMPLES

For most of their long history, the Romans believed in many gods and goddesses. These powerful beings were thought to watch over and control every aspect of daily life. As long as people worshipped the gods, then good things would happen. To make sure of this, people offered gifts to the gods in their homes and at temples.

Houses for the gods

Roman temples were houses for the gods to live in. Don't think of them as being like churches, synagogues, or mosques – because they weren't. While people today worship inside religious buildings, the Romans performed their acts of devotion outside the temples, at altars nearby. The inside of a Roman temple was dark and virtually empty, except for the statue of the god whose temple it was. People believed that the god's spirit lived inside the statue.

Gifts great and small

People sought favours from the gods. In repayment, they

BEFORE THE SACRIFICE OF A BULL, A PRIEST IS SHOWN PURIFYING THE AIR BY BURNING SWEET-SMELLING INCENSE ON A FIRE.

offered gifts, usually anything they could afford, from a cup of wine to an animal such as a pig, a sheep, or a chicken. The bigger the animal, the greater the gift – and gifts didn't come much bigger or more expensive than an ox.

There were rules to follow when animals were slaughtered. Male animals were sacrificed to male gods, and female animals to goddesses. Some gods preferred certain animals, some religious festivals demanded pigs not sheep, and so on.

After the animal had been knocked unconscious, its throat was cut – except if it was a chicken, in which case its neck was wrung. The dead animal was disembowelled and its guts were examined by priests (what a job!) in search of omens. A healthy liver was a good sign, but a diseased liver meant that someone was in for bad luck.

JUPITER, KNOWN BY THE GREEKS AS ZEUS, WAS THE KING OF THE ROMAN GODS.

Household shrines
You didn't have to take a trip to the local temple to offer a gift to the gods. Every Roman family – whether rich or poor – had an altar, or *lararium*, at home. The father, as head of the household, made offerings on behalf of his family. Each morning he said prayers to the household spirits (*lares*) and left bread, fruit, and maybe some wine on the altar.

Happy families
The Romans had a family of 12 main gods and goddesses. What a coincidence, so did the Greeks! How come? Well, the

Romans adopted the Greeks' gods, gave them Roman names, and then worshipped them as their own.

So Zeus, the chief god of the Greeks, became the Roman god Jupiter. Hera, his wife, became the Roman goddess Juno, Athena became Minerva, Ares became Mars, and so on. But it wasn't just Greek gods that the Romans adopted.

THE MEANING OF THIS MOSAIC IS THAT AS TIME ROLLS ON (THE WHEEL), DEATH WILL INEVITABLY COME (THE SKULL).

Isis, an Egyptian goddess, and Mithras, a Persian deity, were also worshipped by some Romans. Instead of stamping out the foreign religions they encountered when they took over new lands, the Romans often incorporated the local beliefs into their own religion. The Romans tolerated people of all religions except those, like Christians, who refused to worship the emperor as well.

It was also thought that the spirits remained in or around their tombs, where they could receive offerings. On the birthday of the dead person or during festivals for the dead,

EACH FAMILY HAD ITS OWN GUARDIAN SPIRIT, OR GENIUS.

Death and beyond

The Romans believed in life after death, but they had various ideas of what it would be like. A common belief was that spirits travelled to a gloomy dark Underworld (land of the dead), which they would reach by crossing the great River Styx. The dead were often buried with a small coin under their tongue. This was to pay Charon, the ferryman who rowed souls across the River Styx.

Once across the vast river, the dead passed Cerberus – a monstrous, three-headed guard-dog who prevented souls from sneaking back over the Styx to the land of the living.

families would visit the tomb and share a meal with them.

Religion of the Christians

In the 1st century CE, in the Roman province of Judea (modern-day Israel, Palestine, and Jordan), a new religion began. It quickly gained many converts, who became known as Christians. They were followers of the teachings of Jesus of

TWO SOULS STEP INTO CHARON'S BOAT TO BE ROWED OVER THE RIVER STYX.

CRUCIFIXION WAS A CRUEL, SHAMEFUL DEATH. THIS SMALL IVORY CARVING, MADE BY CHRISTIANS IN THE 5TH CENTURY CE, DEPICTS THE CRUCIFIXION OF JESUS.

Nazareth. Some Jewish people believed that Jesus was the Messiah, or Christ, sent by God to free them from their Roman oppressors. But the Romans saw Jesus as a threat to law and order and, in about 30 CE, they had Jesus crucified – nailed to a wooden cross and left there to die. The Romans hoped that Jesus's death would settle the matter. But his followers stayed

together, and within a few years a cult had grown up around his memory.

Treated like criminals

By the middle of the 1st century CE, the new religion (Christianity) had reached Rome. Christians were seen as a threat, because their belief in one supreme god challenged the Roman belief in many gods. Rome persecuted Christians who would not worship other gods. Christians were forced to hold their meetings in secret. Rumours

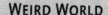

WEIRD WORLD
DID CHRISTIANS DIE IN THE COLOSSEUM? MAYBE, MAYBE NOT. CONTRARY TO POPULAR BELIEF, THERE IS NO EVIDENCE THAT CHRISTIANS WERE EVER KILLED THERE.

spread that they were involved in criminal activities. When a large part of Rome was destroyed by fire in 64 CE, Emperor Nero blamed the Christians for starting it. From then on, a new spectacle was seen in the city. Nero rounded up Christians and had them executed – some were tied to posts, covered in pitch, and set on fire. These human torches burned through the night in the grounds of Nero's palace. He treated others like common criminals and had them either beheaded or thrown to the beasts in the city's arena (a wooden one that existed until the Colosseum was built some years later).

However, this persecution had little effect in curbing the spread of the Christian religion. In time, it proved stronger even than the might of Rome itself.

IN THIS IMAGINATIVE PAINTING, MADE IN THE 1800S, CHRISTIANS ARE KILLED BY WILD ANIMALS IN A ROMAN ARENA.

DECLINE AND FALL

Nothing lasts forever. Not the cruel Colosseum, not the gory games, not even the mighty Roman Empire. From the middle of the 3rd century CE, Rome was struggling to keep out the barbarian tribes that were attacking the frontiers of its territory. To make things worse, emperors and would-be emperors were constantly fighting among themselves. And as for the Christians... well, they just wouldn't go away.

Historic moment

The Battle of the Milvian Bridge, fought outside the city of Rome in October, 312 CE, was a turning point in Roman history. At this battle, Constantine, the Western emperor, defeated his rival Maxentius, emperor of Italy. Before the battle, Constantine had a vision in which the Christian god showed a cross to him and said, "In this sign, conquer!" He believed that the god of the Christians had come to his aid. In gratitude, Constantine allowed Christians to worship as they wished. The days of persecution were over, and the first Christian churches were built in Rome.

EMPEROR CONSTANTINE STOPPED THE PERSECUTION OF CHRISTIANS. HE STARTED TO FOLLOW CHRISTIAN WAYS HIMSELF.

Goodbye gladiators

As more and more Romans began to reject their gods for the Christian god, people also grew unhappy with the brutal games still being staged at the Colosseum.

In 326 CE, Constantine decided to put an end to criminals being condemned to fight to the death in the arena – but that wasn't the end of gladiators altogether. Constantine still allowed people to celebrate his rule with gladiatorial games. However, the "golden age" of gladiators had come to an end.

By 391 CE, under Emperor Theodosius, all forms of pagan (pre-Christian) sacrifice had been banned and temples to the old gods closed. Then, in 399 CE, the gladiatorial schools were shut down by Emperor Honorius. The final nail in the gladiators' coffin came in about 400 CE. The story goes that Almachius, a Christian monk, ran into the Colosseum's arena and tried to separate two gladiators. He was killed either by the angry crowd or by the gladiators on the orders of the Roman officials. Honorius was so disgusted by this that he banned gladiator shows forever, although animal hunts carried on for another 200 years.

THE ABANDONED COLOSSEUM BECAME A RUIN. ITS STONES WERE CARTED AWAY TO MAKE NEW BUILDINGS ELSEWHERE IN ROME.

Beginning of the end

By the late 4th century CE, barbarian tribes, such as the Visigoths and Vandals, were moving into Roman territory. Legions were recalled from the farthest outposts of the empire to defend Rome, but they couldn't stop the Visigoths from destroying much of the city in 410 CE. The empire was falling apart.

A New Rome

In 476 CE, the last Western emperor, Romulus Augustulus, was overthrown by a Germanic chieftain, Odoacer, who made himself king of Italy. The 16-year-old Romulus entered the history books as the last true emperor of Rome.

Roman ways carried on for several hundred years in the eastern part of the empire, where a "New Rome" had been built, named Constantinople (now Istanbul, in modern-day Turkey). But one thing had gone forever – gladiators.

ALARIC, KING OF THE VISIGOTHS, ENTERS ROME WITH HIS WARRIORS IN 410 CE.

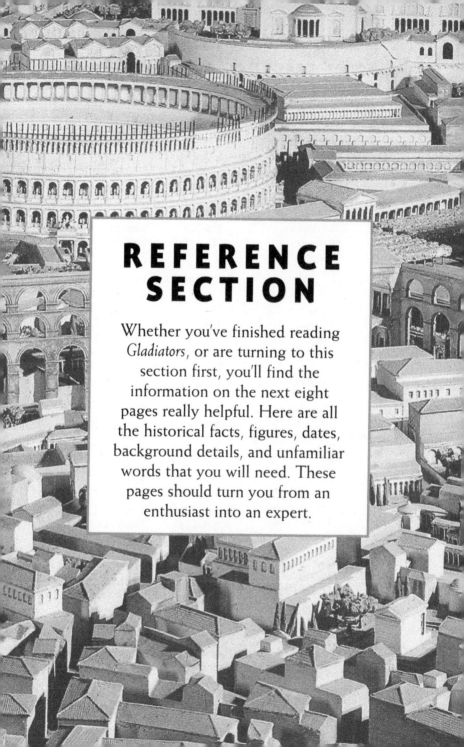

REFERENCE
SECTION

Whether you've finished reading
Gladiators, or are turning to this
section first, you'll find the
information on the next eight
pages really helpful. Here are all
the historical facts, figures, dates,
background details, and unfamiliar
words that you will need. These
pages should turn you from an
enthusiast into an expert.

THE EMPERORS OF ROME

This list names many (but not all) of the men who called themselves emperors of Rome, and the dates of their reigns. At certain times in Rome's history, two or more men claimed the title of emperor at the same time. There were rare times when there was no clear emperor at all. After the empire split in 284 CE, there were usually separate emperors for the Eastern and Western Empires.

Julio-Claudian dynasty

27 BCE–14 CE	Augustus
14–37	Tiberius
37–41	Caligula
41–54	Claudius
54–68	Nero

Civil war of 69 CE

68–69	Galba
69	Vitellius
69	Otho

Flavian dynasty

69–79	Vespasian
79–81	Titus
81–96	Domitian

Nerva/Antonine dynasty

96–98	Nerva
98–117	Trajan
117–138	Hadrian
138–161	Antoninus Pius
161–180	Marcus Aurelius
161–169	Lucius Verus
180–192	Commodus

Civil war of 193 CE

193	Pertinax
193	Didius Julianus
193–194	Pescennius Niger
193–194	Clodius Albinus

Severan dynasty

193–211	Septimius Severus
211–217	Caracalla
211	Geta
217–218	Macrinus
218	Diadumenianus
218–222	Elagabalus
222–235	Severus Alexander

Time of chaos

235–238	Maximinus Thrax
238	Gordian I / Gordian II
238	Pupienus / Balbinus
238–244	Gordian III
244–249	Philip the Arab
249–251	Decius
251–253	Trebonianus Gallus
253	Aemilius Aemilianus
253–260	Valerian
253–268	Gallienus
268–270	Claudius II
270	Quintillus
270–275	Aurelian
275–276	Tacitus
276	Florianus
276–282	Probus
282–283	Carus
283–284	Numerian
283–285	Carinus
284–285	Julian I

Empire divided between east and west

284–305	Diocletian (East)
286–308	Maximian (West)
305–306	Constantius I (West)
305–311	Galerius (East)
306–307	Severus II (West)
306–312	Maxentius (West)

310–313	Maximius (East)	**Last emperors**	
308–324	Licinius (West)	457–461	Majorian (West)
		457–474	Leo (East)
House of Constantine		461–465	Severus III (West)
(empire reunited)		467–472	Anthemius (West)
306–337	Constantine I	472	Olybrius (West)
337–340	Constantine II	473–474	Glycerius (West)
337–350	Constans	474–480	Julius Nepos (West)
337–361	Constantius II	475–476	Romulus Augustulus
360–363	Julian II		(West)
364–365	Jovian		

House of Valentinian

364–375	Valentinian I (West)
364–378	Valens (East)
367–383	Gratian (West)
375–392	Valentinian II (West)

Other claimants to the title

From the 3rd century CE, many other men claimed to be emperor, sometimes ruling whole regions until they were toppled. Here are a few of them.

House of Theodosius

379–395	Theodosius I	260–269	Postumus
	(sole emperor)	269	Marius
393–408	Arcadius (East)	268–271	Victorinus
395–423	Honorius (West)	271–274	Tetricus
402–450	Theodosius II (East)	286–293	Carausius
423–425	Johannes (West)	350–353	Magnentius
425–455	Valentinian III (West)	360–366	Procopius
450–457	Marcian (East)	380–388	Magnus Maximus
455	Petronius Maximus	392–394	Eugenius
	(West)	407–411	Constantine III
		409–411	Maximus
455–456	Avitus (West)	411–413	Jovinus

GLADIATOR WHO'S WHO

Andabata ("blind-fighter")
An *andabata* wore a helmet which covered the eyes, so that they could not see their opponent, also an *andabata*. *Andabatae* were not trained gladiators, but condemned criminals or volunteers, made to fight each other to the death. The bloodthirsty public thought it was funny to watch them slashing wildly at the empty air with their swords.

Bestiarius ("beast fighter")
Someone condemned to fight, or be killed by, wild animals in an amphitheatre. The name was also given to the assistants who looked after the animals.

Crupellarius (meaning unknown)
The *crupellarius*, a type of gladiator from Gaul, was completely covered in metal plate armour, like a medieval knight. A *crupellarius* was slow moving, but hard to wound or kill.

Dimachaerus ('holding two knives")
The *dimachaerus* was a skilled fighter, who fought with a sword or knife in both hands.

Eques ("horse rider")
Fought on horseback with a 2-m (6-ft) lance and a sword. An *eques* carried a round shield, and wore a tunic and a helmet. The mounted gladiator's lower legs and sword arm were guarded by wrappings, and for a fair fight, it was always a fight between a pair of *equites*.

Essedarius ("war-chariot fighter")
Fought from a lightweight, two-wheeled war chariot, like the warriors Julius Caesar fought in Britain. As in British chariot warfare, there may have been two people in each vehicle, a fighter, armed with spears, and a driver.

Gallus ("Gaul")
An early type of gladiator, the *gallus* was a heavily armoured fighter who had a long, slashing sword, like the warriors of Gaul, and a large shield. After Gaul became part of the Roman Empire, the *gallus* fell out of fashion.

Hoplomachus ("shield-fighter")
One of the most heavily armoured fighters, these gladiators wore greaves (metal leg-guards) to protect their lower legs, and covered their right arm and thighs with padded fabric wrappings. A *hoplomachus* wore a helmet to protect their head and face, carried a tiny round shield, and fought with a lance as well as a short sword.

Laquerarius ("noose-fighter")
Fought with a lasso in one hand and a sword in the other.

Myrmillo ("fish")
The name *myrmillo* came from the fighter's big helmet which, in early years, had a distinctive fish-crest. *Myrmillones* carried a sword and a large shield, and although they had a bare chest, their sword arm and legs were protected with fabric wrappings. Their usual opponents were the *thraex* or *hoplomachus*.

Paegniarius ("comic-fighter")
A clown whose job was to entertain the audience with mock fights during intervals. *Paegniarii* wore no armour, and fought each other with whips or wooden swords.

Provocator ("challenger")
Was armed like an early Roman legionary, with a large rectangular shield and a short straight-edged sword. These fighters had a greave on their left leg, a helmet with a visor and two feathers, and an arm-guard on their sword arm. The *provocator* was the only gladiator to wear a breastplate.

Retiarius ("net-fighter")
A lightly armed, fast-moving fighter who did not wear a helmet. *Retiarii* fought with a net, a three-pronged

trident, and a long dagger. Their only armour was an arm guard (manica) and shoulder guard (galerus) protecting the left arm. Apart from a loincloth, they were naked. This gladiator used the net to catch an opponent, who was usually a *secutor*. The *retiarius's* net was weighted with small pieces of lead, which made it spread out easier and quicker when thrown at a *secutor*.

Sagittarius ("archer")
Fought from horseback with a powerful bow, which fired arrows over distances of up to 200 m (660 ft).

Samnite
The oldest type of gladiator, the Samnite was named after an Italian people conquered by the Romans in 290 BCE. These fighters were armed like Samnite warriors, with a rectangular shield, a greave on the left leg, a straight sword, and a helmet decorated with feathers.

Scissor ("cutter")
Apart from the name, almost nothing is known about this gladiator's arms or armour. There is one image of a fighter whose forearm is encased in a metal tube with a curved blade at the end, like the hooks worn by pirates in stories. Perhaps this gladiator was a Scissor.

Secutor ("chaser")
Secutores wore an egg-shaped helmet with two small eye holes designed to protect them from their usual opponents *retiarii*. These gladiators'

smooth helmet would not get caught in the *retiarius's* net, and the eye holes prevented the prongs of the trident blinding their eyes. A *secutor* carried a sword and a long rectangular shield.

Tertiarius ("third fighter")
Sometimes three gladiators were matched against each other. The first two would fight, only for the winner to be met by the third, the *tertiarius*.

Thraex ("Thracian")
The *thraex's* equipment was based on that of the warriors of Thrace, north of the Black Sea. Like real Thracians, a *thraex* carried a short curved sword and a small, round shield. Because these fighters' carried small shields, they had extra body protection, with greaves on both legs and a manica on their right arm. They wore a broad-brimmed helmet topped with a crest of a griffin, a mythical creature, part eagle and part lion, thought to live in Thrace.

Veles ("skirmisher")
Fought with a spear attached to a leash, so that after it was thrown it could be pulled back.

Venator ("hunter")
Hunted wild animals in the arena, armed with a bow and arrow, sword or a spear. *Venatores* wore no armour, and often worked in pairs, assisted by *bestiarii*.

GODS AND GODDESSES

This list names the major Roman gods and goddesses, and also some of the many minor ones. The 12 major deities are indicated by an asterisk (*).

Apollo *
God of prophecy and healing
Greek name – Apollo

Aesculapius
God of healing
Greek name – Asclepius

Bacchus
God of wine
Greek name – Dionysos

Ceres *
Goddess of agriculture
Greek name – Demeter

Cupid
God of love
Greek name – Eros

Diana *
Goddess of the moon and hunting
Greek name – Artemis

Dis (also called Pluto)
God of the Underworld
Greek name – Hades

Faunus
God of fertility
Greek name – Pan

Hercules
God of bravery, male strength, and victory
Greek name – Herakles

Janus
God of doorways
An entirely Roman god

Juno *
Goddess of women and marriage, queen of the gods, wife of Jupiter
Greek name – Hera

Jupiter *
God of the sky, king of the gods, and protector of the Roman state
Greek name – Zeus

Mars *
God of war
Greek name – Ares

Mercury *
God of messengers, travellers, and business
Greek name – Hermes

Minerva *
Goddess of wisdom
Greek name – Athena

Mithras
God of light
Originally from Persia (Iran)

Neptune *
God of the oceans and earthquakes
Greek name – Poseidon

Proserpine
Goddess of the Underworld
Greek name – Persephone

Roma
Goddess of Rome, and protectress of the Roman Empire

Saturn
God of time
Greek name – Cronos

Uranus
God of the sky
Greek name – Ouranos

Venus *
Goddess of love
Greek name – Aphrodite

Vesta *
Goddess of the home and hearth
Greek name – Hestia

Vulcan *
God of fire and blacksmiths
Greek name – Hephaestus

ANCIENT ROME TIMELINE

c.1000 BCE
First villages on the hills of Rome.

753 BCE
Legendary founding of Rome.

c.753–509 BCE
Rome is ruled by kings.

509 BCE
Last king is overthrown, Roman
Republic begins.

390 BCE
Rome is ransacked by Gauls.

264 BCE
First gladiatorial contest in Rome.

264–146 BCE
Wars against Carthage, North Africa.

214–146 BCE
Wars against Greece.

73–71 BCE
Spartacus, a gladiator, leads
a rebellion of 70,000 slaves
against Rome.

58–51 BCE
Julius Caesar conquers Gaul.

44 BCE
After winning a civil war, Julius
Caesar is declared dictator for life.
A few weeks later, he is assassinated.

27 BCE
Roman Republic ends. Octavian
becomes the first Roman emperor
(Augustus). Roman Empire begins.

43 CE
Conquest of Britain begins.

60 CE
Queen Boudicca leads a rebellion in
Britain against the Roman invaders.

64 CE
Fire destroys much of Rome. Nero
begins the persecution of Christians.

68–69 CE
After Nero's death, power struggles
lead to civil war.

79 CE
Destruction of Roman towns by the
eruption of the volcano Vesuvius.

80 CE
Colosseum opens in Rome.

c.120 CE
Roman Empire at its greatest extent.

120–128 CE
Hadrian's Wall is built in Britain.

271 CE
Wall is built around Rome.

284 CE
Roman Empire splits into Eastern
and Western parts.

313 CE
Constantine, Rome's first Christian
emperor, allows Christians –
previously punished as criminals –
to worship freely.

326 CE
Constantine ends gladiatorial combat
as a sentence for crime.

330 CE
Constantinople (Istanbul) becomes
the "New Rome" in the east – the
capital of the Roman world.

c.400 CE
Last known gladiatorial contest at
the Colosseum.

410 CE
Rome is ransacked by Goths.

476 CE
Abdication of Romulus Augustulus,
last emperor of the Western Empire.

476–1453 CE
Eastern Empire flourishes for 1,000
years, until Constantinople is
conquered by the Turks.

GLOSSARY

Amphitheatre
An open-air building for shows.

Amphora
A storage pot for wine or oil.

Aqueduct
A bridge for carrying water.

Arena
The floor area of an amphitheatre. Arena means "sand" in Latin.

Atrium
The entrance area of a Roman house.

Auxiliary
A soldier from a Roman province.

Ballista
A stone-throwing catapult.

Barbarian
According to the Romans, any person from outside the Roman world.

Basilica
A large public building housing law courts, offices, and shops.

Bestiarius
A performer who tormented animals in the arena.

Bulla
A lucky charm worn by children.

Calculator
A teacher who taught maths.

Centurion
The commander of a century.

Century
A company of 80–100 soldiers.

Circus
A race-track.

Citizen
Originally a man born in Rome to Roman parents. Eventually, people across the empire were granted the right to call themselves citizens.

Clavi
The stripes on Roman clothes.

Cohort
A unit of 480 soldiers in a legion.

Consul
The most senior government official.

Crucifixion
A form of execution in which a person was nailed or tied to a cross or tree.

Domus
A house in a town.

Editor
A wealthy person who sponsored a gladiatorial show.

Emperor
The ruler of the Roman world.

Empire
(1) The extent of all the provinces ruled by the Romans. (2) The time when Rome was ruled by emperors.

Etruscans
People in Italy, north of Rome, who flourished before the Romans.

Forum
The square in the middle of a Roman town, which was used for markets, politics, and processions.

Genius
A protecting spirit.

Gladiator
A highly trained fighter, named after the *gladius*, a type of sword.

Gladius
A short sword used by a gladiator.

Graffiti
Words scratched or painted onto a wall or other surface.

Grammaticus
A teacher who taught grammar.

Greave
A metal protector for the lower leg.

Lanista
An owner-trainer of gladiators.

Lararium
A small altar in a private house.
Lares
Spirits who protected the household.
Latin
The language of the Romans.
Latium
The homeland of the Romans
in Italy.
Legate
The commanding officer of a legion.
Legion
An army division, usually of
4,800 soldiers.
Legionary
A soldier belonging to
a legion.
Litterator
A teacher of reading and writing.
Ludus
A school for training gladiators.
Mosaic
A picture made of stone, pottery, or
glass cubes.
Palla
A shawl worn by women.
Papyrus
An Egyptian water-reed from which
writing paper was made.
Peristylium
The garden of a Roman house.
Pilum
The javelin used by Roman soldiers.
Praetorian Guard
The emperor's personal army.
Province
A territory of the Roman Empire.
Pugio
The dagger used by Roman soldiers.
Republic
A state or country governed by
officials elected by the people.
Rhetor
A teacher who taught public speaking.

Rudis
The wooden sword given to gladiators
on their retirement from the arena.
Senate
The group of elected nobles who
governed Rome.
Senator
An official, a member of the Senate.
Socci
Slippers worn indoors.
Stola
The main garment worn by women.
Strigil
A scraper used to clean the body.
Stylus
A writing pen.
Thermae
A Roman bath-house.
Toga
Robe worn by Roman male citizens
for important occasions.
Tribune
A middle-ranking officer in a legion.
Triclinium
The dining-room of a private house.
Tunica
A shirt-like undergarment.
Venatio
An animal show.
Venator
An animal-hunter.
Villa
A large house in the country.
Vomitoria
Entrances and exits at an arena.

INDEX

ACKNOWLEDGMENTS

The publisher would like to thank the following people for their help with making the book:
Marcus James for initial design concept; Amanda Wyatt for editorial assistance; Surya Sankash Sarangi for picture research; Dean Price for jacket design; Rakesh Kumar, Priyanka Sharma, and Saloni Singh for the jacket; and Chris Bernstein for the index.

Illustration by: Russell Barnett 18bl.

Additional photography by: Joe Cornish, Mike Dunning, Simon James, Dave King, Liz McAulay, Karl Shone, Lin White, Alan Williams.
